Best Hikes With
CHILDREN®
Around Sacramento

D1041028

Best Hikes With
CHILDREN
Around Sacramento

By Bill McMillon
with Kevin McMillon

THE
MOUNTAINEERS

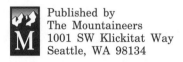

Published by
The Mountaineers
1001 SW Klickitat Way
Seattle, WA 98134

©1993 by Bill McMillon and Kevin McMillon

0 9 8 7 6
6 5 4 3 2

Published simultaneously in Canada by Douglas & McIntyre, Ltd., 1615 Venables Street, Vancouver, B.C. V5L 2H1

Published simultaneously in Great Britain by Cordee, 3a DeMontfort Street, Leicester, England LE1 7HD

Manufactured in the United States of America

Edited by Kris Fulsaas
Maps by Beth Duke
All photographs by Bill McMillon
Cover design by Watson Graphics
Book layout by Constance Bollen
Typography by The Mountaineers Books

Cover photograph: Enjoying an energy break at the top

Library of Congress Cataloging in Publication Data
McMillon, Bill, 1942–
    Best hikes with children around Sacramento / Bill McMillon with Kevin McMillon.
        p.   cm.
    Includes index.
    ISBN 0-89886-278-7
    1. Hiking—California—Sacramento Metropolitan Area—Guidebooks.
2. Outdoor recreation for children—California—Guidebooks. 3. Sacramento Metropolitan Area—Guidebooks. I. McMillon, Kevin, 1982– . II. Title.
GV199.42.C22S235   1993
796.5'1'0979453--dc20   93-2010
                                                                  CIP

To park rangers everywhere—many thanks

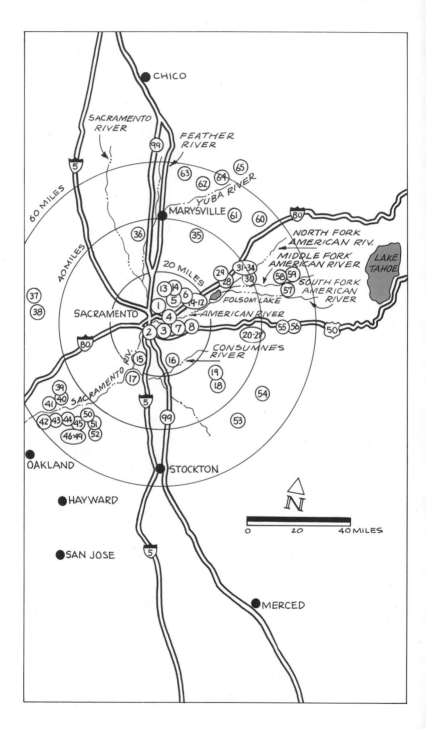

Contents

Relaxing at the top

Introduction

Working on this book was a homecoming of sorts for me, but to a home only dimly remembered as I began to search for hikes to include in this guide. I attended high school in Sacramento in the late 1950s, and at that time there was a large field behind our house where jackrabbits and birds were abundant. Sheep grazed where Country Club Plaza, Country Club Center, and Arden Fair Mall now sit. Hop fields covered the land to the south of the American River; the banks of the river itself were wild places where we had to bush-whack when we wanted to go beyond the few access points, and the newly built Folsom Dam was a day's trip into the country.

Between the two ends of Fair Oaks Boulevard (one where the bridge crossed the river at the end of J Street and the other where the Fair Oaks Bridge led to Folsom Boulevard and US 50) no bridge crossed the American River.

Today vast subdivisions have replaced the hop fields; sheep don't graze within 20 miles of downtown Sacramento; four bridges cross the American River between J Street and Folsom (a new bridge has replaced the old Fair Oaks Bridge), and there are few open spaces between Sacramento and Folsom Dam.

It was with trepidation that I began to search for places to hike near downtown and the outlying suburbs. I feared that I would have to go miles beyond the population center, and would then find only a few good hikes for families with children.

What I found was a very pleasant surprise. Large parks have been set aside in the region for those who love the outdoors, and several of these have nature areas where families can enjoy short hikes. The 23-mile-long American River Parkway runs from Discovery Park at the confluence of the Sacramento and American rivers to Nimbus Dam, where it joins with trails in the Folsom State Recreation Area that extend all the way to Auburn along the reservoirs and river. The American River Parkway has become an outstanding example of how an urban area can utilize waterways for recreational purposes. This network offers an astounding amount of hiking, and Sacramento County has developed a number of parks along the parkway that offer hikes away from the river's edge.

When these centrally located trails are added to those in the foothills of the Sierra Nevada, and along the waterways and reservoirs of both the foothill and delta regions, Sacramento residents have a wide variety of hikes to choose from as they escape from the confines of downtown or the suburbs. If an easy evening stroll is all they want, there is no better place than the American River Parkway. For birdwatchers, the Sacramento/San Joaquin Delta region and the wildlife refuges to the north are among the premier birding sites in the United States. The steep ravines and oak-covered slopes of the Sierra Nevada foothills offer strenuous hikes for those who want exercise along with their outings. And the many man-made lakes and reservoirs in the canyons of the foothills provide long hikes along serrated shorelines where wildlife is abundant.

Beyond the delta toward the San Francisco Bay Area, the ridges and peaks of Contra Costa County are within an easy hour's drive from downtown Sacramento, and offer outstanding vistas not available in the flatlands of the Central Valley.

This guide describes day and overnight hikes within a 60-mile radius of Sacramento that you can explore with your family, from young children to grandparents. Some are short hikes of 0.5 mile or less for even the youngest and oldest, while others are more than 5 miles long for those who want to both enjoy nature and engage in pleasurable, vigorous physical activity.

HIKING WITH CHILDREN

Some children can't resist stopping to wade along a slow-moving stream, or watch an acorn woodpecker drill holes in a pine tree. Others want to push on up a trail to reach a hidden beach or an exposed mountain peak as quickly as possible. Each enjoys hikes in his or her own special way, and does so with great bursts of enthusiasm. And parents find such enthusiasm contagious.

Even the most enthusiastic child sometimes needs a little added encouragement to make it through a day's hike, however, and the following guidelines can help you get through those times—making hikes fun for all.

Know What Your Family Prefers on a Hike

Each family has its own ideas about hiking. While some decide on a destination, and concentrate on reaching it, others are more spontaneous, and reaching a particular destination is of only secondary importance. The same is true for members of a family. Some like to surge ahead along the trail to a rest stop where they may dawdle for a while; others like to take a more leisurely pace along the trail with shorter rest stops.

After an outing or two, you will know what your family prefers, and you can plan future trips with those preferences in mind.

Plan a Destination

Talk about your destination before you begin hiking, and let everyone know what there is to be seen and explored along the way. Find a creek, a particularly interesting tree, or an outstanding vista, and plan to stop there. You may not make all the planned stops, but your family will have markers to help measure their progress during the hike.

You don't have to be intimately familiar with a trail to do this; you can find information in this guide, or from other sources, to help plan a hike.

Plan for Nourishment and Rest

Always carry plenty of water, or other liquids, and snacks, even on short hikes. These can be used as incentives when the trail gets steep, or the day gets warm, and your charges begin dragging. A simple reminder that "we will stop at the next shady spot to have some water and energy food" will give all the impetus to continue along the trail.

Also, remember to take plenty of "energy" stops so no one on the hike gets overly tired.

"Adopt" a Child for the Day

You may want to bring a friend or friends along on the hike so each child has a companion with whom to share discoveries and rest stops.

Accentuate the Positive

Praise such as "you certainly did a good job coming up that hill" is important to children, and it lets them know that you are aware of how much effort they are putting into an activity.

If a child shows signs of slowing down on a difficult section of a trail, distractions and patience—casually observing some trailside plants or rocks as your child overtakes you, or a "look at that soaring hawk"—will help with progress along a trail.

Tired Children

While most parents have a good idea of how far their children can hike, and plan their outings with those limitations in mind, there are times when the best-laid plans go awry.

There are ways to overcome what are seemingly insurmountable problems, though. In the mid-1970s my wife and I took our four-year-old on a camping trip to Point Reyes National Seashore with a group of high school students. All went well until the last day of the trip, when we discovered that we had neglected to study thoroughly a topographical map of the area. The first portion of the trail from Wildcat Canyon to Bear Valley was a rugged climb, one that no four-year-old could make without help.

Even with the assistance of several teenagers who carried one of our packs and most of our supplies, we began the day with trepidation. The first half hour went fine, but drastic measures were soon needed. First, I carried Matt piggyback, but there was obviously a limit to this. He needed some incentive to walk more, and that incentive turned out to be a game of hide-and-seek.

Mary and I used our snack supply, and took turns heading up the trail to hide a goody behind a rock or plant. We then encouraged Matt to scurry up the trail to find them. A successful search was followed by a short energy break while the snack was eaten.

This game got us over the hump, literally, and we made it to our car in a reasonable time. We learned a valuable lesson, however, and ever since we choose hikes that take in the abilities of *everyone in the family*, checking out the entire trail on a topographic map if we haven't hiked it before.

Of the many ways to avoid such problems on dayhikes, the best is to develop contingency plans for turning back short of your original destination. To help you with your hike plans, I have included "turn-around" sites for longer one-way hikes, and the "point-of-no-return" for longer loop hikes where it will be shorter to continue than to go back.

Have Fun Along the Way

Hikes should be fun. Enjoy yourself and help others enjoy themselves. Explore the area along the trail, and experience the sights, sounds, and smells of nature as you move along the trail. Remember, your goal isn't necessarily to reach a specific destination, but to have an enjoyable outing with your family where your children learn to enjoy and respect their natural environment.

TRAIL ETIQUETTE

Regardless of how well you plan a hike, or how well behaved your children are, there are times when things don't go right. And there are certain rules of behavior that are expected of all hikers, whether they are children or adults.

The Call of Nature

All the suggestions of "go to the bathroom now, there isn't one on the trail" won't prevent an occasional crisis when your child has to go, and immediately. If the child merely has to urinate, take him or her at least 200 feet from any trail or creek. If your child must defecate, dig a hole at least 6 inches deep in which to bury the feces. The used toilet paper (and you should always carry a small roll) should be wrapped in a plastic bag, and carried out for disposal.

Uncontrolled Children

Hiking should be fun, but uncontrolled children who run rapidly around blind trail curves, yell loudly, and destroy plants and wildlife aren't fun for anyone. Always set some firm ground rules for your children and any friends brought along on a hike.

Talking about these rules well beforehand lets everyone develop a positive approach toward how to act in the wilderness. Rather than just talking about what not to do, help your children see what others do that is undesirable, and emphasize that "good hikers" don't do those things. By the time you get on the trail they will be on the lookout for such negative behavior, and will need little encouragement to avoid it themselves.

One rule that is frequently violated by children is cutting across switchbacks. Children love to slip and slide down a hill as they run ahead of others, but the practice is devastating to the hillsides, and often leads to washed-out trails. A reminder of the damage caused by this, along with a few examples of damage pointed out on the trail, is usually sufficient.

Family Pets

Don't bring them, even if the rules of the trail say you can. Although Rover may like outings as much as other members of the family, most trails just aren't appropriate for pets, especially if you want to enjoy the plants and animals along the way.

Fires

No fires should ever be built in any of the parks mentioned here except in designated sites at campgrounds and picnic areas. This is extremely important, because most of the trails in this guide are in and near habitats that become extremely volatile during the hot, dry months between May and October. Many parks even have rules against smoking on their trails during dry summer months.

Trail Right-of-Way

While hikers have as much right to the use of the trails in this guide as any other group, simple courtesy and a sense of safety say that hikers should give the right-of-way to mountain bikers and horseback riders. When you hear them coming, step off the trail, wait for them to pass, and avoid any loud noises or sudden movement as they do.

Leave Nothing but Footprints; Take Nothing but Photos

Most of the hikes in this guide are in regional, state, or national parks, all of which have rules about collecting or destroying plants, animals, and other natural items. Help your children understand these rules, and why they exist. If you are unsure of what the rules are for any park where you plan to hike, contact the local ranger for information, which they are always glad to furnish.

This is an opportunity to develop a wilderness ethic for your family by emphasizing how parks have been set aside for all to enjoy, and that destruction of plants and animals (and collecting often has the same results as heedless destruction), as well as unsightly littering, defeats that purpose.

ENJOYING NATURE

While hiking can be an end unto itself, most children like to investigate the ins and outs of the world around them, and that includes sites along trails. A creek becomes something more than just a body of water to be crossed. It becomes a place to investigate, a place where smooth, round rocks can be skipped across large pools, where insect larvae can be discovered under slimy bottom rocks, where frogs can be found in creekside vegetation, and where feet can be soaked as energy food is consumed.

The same is true of trees, boulders, and hillsides. All provide many attractions to your children, and you can utilize this interest to introduce the study of nature, and you can do so in a sharing way.

Sharing, Not Teaching

Let your children share in your interests as you walk along the trail and at rest stops. Point out a wildflower that you like. If your child is interested, discuss where the flower grows, what insects are around it, and other particulars that you can observe—and you can do all of these without ever knowing the flower's name.

You don't have to teach the children anything. They can experience it right along with you. And you can experience anew the delight of investigating a creekbed, tree, or bluff through their eyes.

Use All Your Senses on the Trail

Watch the light fall across a meadow, smell a pine tree, and touch a thistle. Even taste a limestone rock. All these will give you and your children a variety of sensations with which to experience nature.

Getting the Feel of Nature

When your child complains about the trail being hot and dusty, ask how the animals in the area cope with the midday heat, and where they get their refreshments. Suggest that the shade of the forest ahead may bring about a change in mood, and offer a drink or snack to help refresh the spirit as well as the body. Once you get to that shady forest, discuss how the animals that live nearby might enjoy similar breaks during their day.

Relating moods and experiences to the wildlife that lives in the region will help you and your children become more in touch with the natural world, and add immeasurably to your hiking experiences.

Seed pods have a beauty of their own.

With these suggestions, and thoughts of your own, you should be able to find trails in this guide that will give you many hours of pleasant outdoor activity. Go, and enjoy, but first make some prehike preparations.

GETTING READY FOR DAYHIKES

While it is possible to simply get in your car and drive to a hiking trail with no preparation, it is not necessarily wise. A little preparation will make all hikes more enjoyable, and may prevent unnecessary trouble, especially on overnight hikes.

The Ten Essentials

The Mountaineers recommends ten items that should be taken on every hike, whether a day trip or an overnight. When children are involved, and you are particularly intent on making the trip as trouble-free as possible, these "Ten Essentials" may avert disaster.

1. **Extra clothing.** It may rain, the temperature may drop, or wading may be too tempting to pass up. Be sure to include rain gear, extra shoes and socks (especially a pair of shoes that can be used for wading), a warm sweater, and a hat and light gloves.

2. **Extra food.** Extra high-energy snacks are essential for active children and adults. Carry sufficient water in canteens and fanny packs in case no suitable source is available on the trail.

3. **Sunglasses.** Look for a pair that screens UV rays.

4. **Knife.** Chances are you will never need it, but bring one along anyway. A knife with multiple blades, scissors, a bottle opener, and tweezers is a must.

5. **Firestarter—candle or chemical fuel.** If you must build a fire, these are indispensable.

6. **First-aid kit.** Don't forget to include moleskin for blisters, baking soda to apply to stings, any special medication your child might need if he or she is allergic to bee stings or other insect bites, and extra sunscreen.

7. **Matches in a waterproof container.** You can buy these matches in a store that carries hiking and camping gear.

8. **Flashlight.** Check the batteries before you begin your hike.

9. **Map.** Don't assume you'll just "feel" your way to the summit. Maps are important, and I discuss them more later in this introduction.

10. **Compass.** Teach your children how to use it, too.

In addition to these Ten Essentials, the following suggestions will help make hikes more enjoyable.

What to Wear

There is little need for special clothes or shoes for hiking in the Sacramento area. Trails are generally well marked and stable. They don't demand heavy-duty hiking boots and, because we have such an equable climate, specialty clothing is rarely called for.

Active-wear shoes such as those your children wear to school and for playing around home are perfectly adequate. Sneakers, especially high tops, give all the support needed, and have the advantage of being well-broken in. This helps keep blisters to a minimum, thereby avoiding one of the most uncomfortable aspects of hiking.

To enjoy hiking in the Sacramento area, it is important to wear enough of the right kinds of clothing to keep you comfortable in changing weather. This means layers that can be removed and put back on as the day's weather changes from windy and foggy to sunny and warm—and back again. Because hiking is a year-round activity in the area, and there are so many microclimates throughout the region, it is difficult to say exactly what clothing you should carry on any one hike. The only thing certain is that you may need layers of clothes any time of year, on any hike.

Rain gear is generally important only in the winter, with an occasional fall or spring storm, but a hat or cap is useful year-round to protect adults and youth alike from the effects of the sun.

Packs

Not everyone has to have a pack on a dayhike, but children love to carry their own to hold their special items. Adults' day packs should be large enough to carry bulky clothing and extra food and drinks, but youngsters can use either day or fanny packs. The only requirement is that the packs should be large enough for some food, small items such as magnifying glasses, individual drinking containers, and layers of clothing that have been removed.

For overnight hikes, everyone should have a pack large enough to carry extra clothing and a sleeping bag. Older children can also help carry food and cooking utensils.

Other Items

Other items you may want to bring along to help make hikes more fun include lightweight binoculars (one pair per family should do, but some families have several) for looking at birds and animals, as well as scouting the trail ahead, a magnifying glass and insect boxes for short-term viewing of small animals and plants, a lightweight camera for recording the trip, and possibly some nature guides to help identify objects in the field as they are observed. You can use your knife to help dig around in old stumps and under rocks when searching for creepy crawlers.

None of these items is essential for the enjoyment of hikes, but all help you and your family explore the world of nature close-up, and provide activities that can be pursued during rest breaks and eating times.

Tents

Because rain is such an unusual event during the summer months in the Sacramento Valley and the lower foothills of the Sierra Nevada, a tent is not an absolute necessity on overnight trips, but one is recommended. Everyone likes to have privacy while changing clothes, and many younger children fall asleep more easily if they have some shelter surrounding them. There are a number of inexpensive, lightweight tents available at backpacking and outdoor supply stores that are perfectly adequate for short backpacking trips.

A trailside break helps rejuvenate everyone.

Maps

Most of the trails in this book are in developed parks, so you are unlikely to get lost on any of these hikes, although some of the longer ones do take you away from the most heavily traveled areas of the larger parks. A little common sense, a copy of the park brochure, and an awareness of where the trail is, however, should keep you on track.

Topographic maps with contour lines and marked trails aren't strictly necessary, but can be fun and interesting for children. When combined with an inexpensive compass, they can be used to determine your exact position on the trail, as well as provide a new and interesting learning experience.

Topographical maps of the region and compasses, as well as instruction books on how to use them, are sold in most hiking and camping stores in the area.

Food and Drinks

Outings are a good time to let your children have high-energy foods such as candy bars and other sweet snacks as treats. These can be used as motivation to get to that shady tree up the trail where you can stop for a rest, or over the hump to the top of a ridge. You can also take along other foods such as fruit and high-protein foods that the children like for lunch breaks.

Children like to carry some food in their own packs, but you can hold back special treats until they are needed for motivation.

Remember also that one of the "Ten Essentials" is extra food. Whatever you take on the hike, don't skimp. It is always better to carry extra food home than to have hikers become cranky and disagreeable from hunger.

Another item that you absolutely must not skimp on is fluids. Many of the hikes in this guide can be hot and dry during the summer months, and few have drinking water available.

While sugary drinks and sports drinks are fine for replacing lost fluids, never depend solely upon them. On our son Kevin's sixth birthday, we took a group of boys on a long hike, and took along only snack drinks to have with lunch and along the trail. The June day was hot, there was no potable water at the lake, and several of the group complained loudly about their need for "real" water during the 5-mile round trip to the lake and back.

Overnight trips require a little extra planning for food. You need to keep supplies light, but you also want to make sure that what you do take is satisfying and nourishing. Children may be willing to try new foods while camping, but always make sure that you have some family favorites along in case the new foods don't work out.

First Aid and Safety

First aid and safety are generally big items in hiking books, but in reality I have found that my children have less need for first aid on the trail than during a normal day at home.

Nevertheless, my "Ten Essentials" first-aid kit includes large and small Band-Aids, anti-bacterial cream, a squeeze bottle of hydrogen peroxide, a patch of moleskin, some scissors, an athletic bandage, a medicine for relief of insect stings, and some itch medicine. Recently I have also begun carrying a cold wrap, but I must admit this is more for me than for my children.

Though not technically first aid, sunscreen and insect repellent should also be carried. While biting insects aren't a major problem in the area, there are times when mosquitoes and flies can be bothersome, and the repellent helps. Sunscreen is an absolute necessity, especially for those of us who are so fair-skinned that we "burn while on the backside of the moon," because many trails in the region cover long distances where there is little or no shade.

In addition to the normal scrapes and falls that accompany active children, nature also offers several circumstances that are, if not dangers, at least worries that parents must be aware of and caution children about.

Poison Oak, Nettles, and Thistles. These are all plants that can precipitate either an immediate or delayed reaction that causes discomfort, and you should be aware of what these plants look like during various seasons.

Stinging nettles cause a more immediate reaction than poison oak (which generally doesn't appear for two days to two weeks from exposure) and can be quite painful—even excruciatingly so—to children and adults alike. Various types of thistles also cause intense pain and itching to some people.

Itch medicines help with, but don't completely relieve, the discomfort of stinging nettles. The best solution is to avoid contact. If you don't know what the various plants look like, park rangers will be glad to help you identify them, and many parks have signs illustrating poison oak and nettles. If you are hiking in areas such as the delta, where nettles and thistles are abundant, you may want to take along a guidebook with which to make a positive identification.

Stinging Insects. Some areas covered by this guide have a large numbers of stinging insects such as yellow jackets, and these can be scary to children. While their stings are painful, they don't have to be cause for ending a hike. Over-the-counter medicines are available that relieve the discomfort when rubbed on a sting.

Rattlesnakes. Rattlesnakes are another fear of parents, and many trails in this guide are in areas with large populations of rattlers that come out during warm spring and hot summer months. Very few hikers ever see these reclusive animals, though, and a few simple precautions are all that are necessary to avoid a bite:

Never stick your hand down into rocky crevices without first looking. Never climb rock faces where you have to put your hands into holes for handholds. Always watch where you are stepping when you step over logs and rocks. ·

Rattlesnakes are poisonous, and they do occasionally bite people, but their bites are seldom fatal. If, by chance, a member of your hiking party is bitten by a rattlesnake, don't panic. Have the person who was bitten lie down and remain still, and send another member of the group to find a ranger or phone. Let the authorities, whether a ranger or 911, know where the victim is located, and when the bite occurred. With modern medicine, there is little danger if medical attention is given promptly.

Lost and Injured Children. I have tried to emphasize the reality of dangers on trails, but most are minimal. Two dangers, however, stand out above all others, and adults can do much to control them.

The first is injury and death from falls around cliffs. Children love to climb on rocks and cliffs, and have great fun doing so, but this activity can be dangerous. Always check out any rocks where the children are climbing to be sure there are no loose surfaces that may give way under their weight, and only allow them to climb on low cliffs. Falls from high ones are always dangerous, and likely to cause serious injury.

The second danger is of children who stray from the group and become lost and panic-stricken. Search-and-rescue units spend many hours searching for lost children in the region, and members often speak to school and youth groups about how to avoid this lonely and terrifying experience.

First, they advise that everyone carry a loud whistle. Second, they recommend that anyone separated from the group, and unable to gain attention with a whistle, "hug" a tree (or a bush or a boulder). This means the person should sit down next to a tree or bush or boulder, and stay there until found. The only other action the lost person should take is to blow a whistle or shout loudly at regular intervals.

With these simple precautions and preparations, you should find that hiking the trails of the Sacramento region will be a satisfying way to spend family outings.

SOME NOTES ON THE NATURAL HISTORY OF THE SACRAMENTO REGION

A wide variety of plant and animal communities are found around Sacramento. Many hikers enjoy their outings without ever learning anything of significance about either the plants or animals that they may encounter on the trail, but I find that I enjoy my outings a little more when I learn something about the various natural communities, and how the plants and animals interact with each other. For those who want to learn more about the various fauna and flora of the Sacramento region, both the University of California Press and Wilderness Press publish a number of natural history guidebooks that are very useful. The following are a few examples of the flora and fauna that you are likely to see in your wanderings.

Chaparral

Many hills of California are covered by a dense growth of hard-leafed, drought-resistant plants collectively known as chaparral. The plants in this community are well adapted to the long dry summers and wet winters of Northern California, because they tolerate the hot dry spells and protect the hillsides during the wet winter months. In addition, they regenerate very quickly from fires.

The plants in these communities include various species of

Animal homes, such as this trap-door spider hole, are often found at the base of tall grass.

manzanita, which has shiny red bark on its trunk and branches and ranges from low creepers to 15-foot-tall shrubs; ceanothus, sometimes called California lilac, with its large clusters of blue or white flowers; and chamise, a member of the rose family that spreads into almost impenetrable thickets that are 2 to 10 feet high.

Wildflowers

Wildflowers such as California poppy and blue lupine are familiar to everyone who has driven along the highways of Northern California, but there are dozens more native wildflowers that can be identified along the trails in this guide.

Trees

Several species of trees are so common in the region that you will probably encounter at least one species on almost every hike in this book. These include the many species of oak that are native to the region (and it is hard for some people to distinguish between these); various species of exotic eucalyptus (which were brought here from Australia in the nineteenth century); bay, which is also known as California laurel, pepperwood, and myrtle; buckeye, a member of the horse-chestnut family; various pines such as lodgepole and digger; and the many species of willow found along the creeks and rivers of the valley.

Mammals

Raccoon, opossum, gray squirrels, chipmunks, ground squirrels, rabbits, coyote, gray fox, bobcat, and black-tailed deer are some of the more common animals that you are either likely to encounter or observe signs of along the trails. In some parks you may even see signs of bear and cougar, but you're not likely to run into either.

None of these present any danger to hikers, with the possible exception of bear and cougar (and there have been no reports of attacks by either in the area in many years), and children are delighted to see animals in their natural habitat.

Birds

Various hawks, vultures, magpies, jays, and many songbirds are all common in the region, and a bird guide will help you identify the many smaller birds that you will run across on your hikes. The Sacramento Valley is also a prime stopover site for waterfowl and other birds that migrate along the Pacific Flyway.

HOW TO USE THIS GUIDE

The hikes in this guide are located in Contra Costa, Solano, Yolo, Sacramento, San Joaquin, Placer, El Dorado, Amador, Calaveras, Nevada, and Yuba counties, and most are located within county, regional, state, and federal parks and reserves. Most parks provide maps or brochures that describe the trails within their boundaries, and tell something about the natural history of the region. You can obtain these either at the parks or from park district offices. Addresses and phone numbers of park districts are listed at the end of this introduction.

Although most of the trails in the guide are permanent, there is always the possibility that one will be closed because of landslide, fire danger, or other natural condition. In addition, park officials sometimes reroute trails or close them temporarily for other reasons.

You can call the park where you intend to hike to ask about the latest trail conditions and find out if the trail you intend to use is open. If it isn't, you can ask about similar trails nearby and most park officials will gladly help.

The hikes that are included were selected with several thoughts in mind. One was that there be some hikes that anyone, even those barely past the toddler stage and those who are quite elderly, could enjoy. Another was that the majority be moderate hikes from which most families would derive a sense of accomplishment from completing. The last was that some be difficult enough to challenge older children (up to twelve years old) in good physical condition who like to hike.

There are also some overnight hikes included for those families who would like to introduce their children to the joys of backpacking without venturing long distances from home.

The hikes also cover the wide range of natural habitats that exist in the area. Open grasslands, oak woodlands, mixed oak forests, mixed conifer forests, delta, marsh, and riparian habitats are all represented, and you will see a wide variety of flora and fauna as you walk along the trails.

Information blocks for the hikes tell whether the hike is a day trip or overnight, rate its difficulty for children, and give its length, hiking time required, elevation gain, best season for hiking, and recommended map. The descriptions of the hikes include the location and tell something about the natural history of the region covered by the trails.

PARK DISTRICT HEADQUARTERS

The following is a listing of the district headquarters of the local, county, regional, state, and national parks where the hikes in this guide are located. If you have any questions about the conditions of the trails—whether it is too wet or hot or dry to hike in the park, what wildflowers are blooming, et cetera—give them a call. They are always willing to answer questions, or refer you to someone who can.

Many of these park districts charge fees, and offer yearly discount passes to heavy users. You may want to investigate these if you have a favorite region where you plan to hike extensively.

Auburn State Recreation Area
PO Box 1680
Auburn, CA 95603
916-885-4527

Benicia State Recreation Area
First and G Streets
Benicia, CA 94510
707-648-1911

Brannan Island State Recreation Area
Star Route, Box 75A
Rio Vista, CA 94571
916-777-6671

Camanche Lake South Shore
Recreation Area
PO Box 206
Burson, CA 95225
209-763-5178

Consumnes River Preserve
The Nature Conservancy
7100 Desmond Road
Galt, CA 95632
916-686-6982

East Bay Regional Park
District
11500 Skyline Boulevard
Oakland, CA 94619
510-531-9300

Empire Mine State Historic
Park
10791 E. Empire Street
Grass Valley, CA 95945
916-273-8522

Folsom Lake State Recreation
Area
7806 Folsom–Auburn Road
Folsom, CA 95630
916-988-0205

Grizzly Island Game Refuge
2548 Grizzly Island Road
Suisun City, CA 94585
707-425-3828

Indian Grinding Rocks State
Historic Park
14881 Pine Grove–Volcano
Road
Pine Grove, CA 95665
209-296-7488

Lake Berryessa Recreation
Office
PO Box 9332
Spanish Flat Station
Napa, CA 94558
707-966-2111

Marshall Gold Discovery State
Historic Park
PO Box 265
Coloma, CA 95613
916-622-3470

Mount Diablo State Park
PO Box 250
Diablo, CA 94528
510-837-2525

New Hogan Lake
2713 Hogan Dam Road
Valley Springs, CA 95252
209-772-1343

Pardee Lake Recreation Area
4900 Stoney Creek Road
Ione, CA 95640
209-772-1472

Placer County Parks Division
11476 C Avenue
Auburn, CA 95603
916-889-7750

Sacramento County Department
of Parks and Recreation
3711 Branch Center Road
Sacramento, CA 95827
916-366-2066

Sly Park Recreation Area
PO Box 577
Pollock Pines, CA 95726
916-644-2545

Solano County Farmlands and
Open Space Foundation
PO Box 115
Fairfield, CA 94533
707-428-7580

South Yuba River Recreation
Area
Bureau of Land Management,
Folsom Resource Area
63 Natoma Street
Folsom, CA 95630
916-985-4474

Spenceville Wildlife Area
California Department of Fish
and Game, Region 2
1701 Nimbus Road, Suite A
Rancho Cordova, CA 95819
916-355-7010

Tahoe National Forest
Highway 49 and Coyote Street
Nevada City, CA 95959
916-265-4531

A NOTE ABOUT SAFETY

Safety is an important concern in all outdoor activities. No guide-book can alert you to every hazard or anticipate the limitations of every reader. Therefore, the descriptions of roads, trails, routes, and natural features in this book are not representations that a particular place or excursion will be safe for your party. When you follow any of the routes described in this book, you assume responsibility for your own safety. Under normal conditions, such excursions require the usual attention to traffic, road and trail conditions, weather, terrain, the capabilities of your party, and other factors. Keeping informed on current conditions and exercising common sense are the keys to a safe, enjoyable outing.

The Mountaineers

KEY TO SYMBOLS

 Dayhikes. These are hikes that can be completed in a single day. While some trips allow camping, only a few require it.

 Easy trails. These are relatively short, smooth, gentle trails suitable for small children and first-time hikers.

 Moderate trails. Most of these are 2 to 4 miles in total distance and feature up to 500 feet elevation gain. The trail may be rough and uneven. Hikers might wear lug-soled boots and should be sure to carry the Ten Essentials.

 Difficult trails. These are often rough, with considerable elevation gain or distance to travel. They are suitable for older or experienced children. Lug-soled boots and the Ten Essentials are standard equipment.

 Hikable. The best times of year to hike each trail are indicated by the following symbols: flower—spring; sun—summer; leaf—fall; snowflake—winter.

 Driving directions. These paragraphs tell you how to get to the trailheads.

 Turnarounds. These are places, mostly along moderate trails, where families can cut their hikes short, yet still have a satisfying outing. Turnarounds usually offer picnic opportunities, views, or special attractions.

 Cautions. These mark potential hazards—cliffs, stream or highway crossings, and the like—where close supervision of children is strongly recommended.

 Environmental close-ups. These highlight special environmental elements along the trail and help children learn about and respect nature.

LEGEND

═══	PRIMARY ROAD OR FREEWAY
▬▬▬	STREET OR SECONDARY ROAD
=====	UNPAVED ROAD OR FIRE ROAD
••••••	HIKING TRAIL (DIRT OR GRAVEL)
•—•—•	PAVED TRAIL
– – – –	OTHER TRAIL
Ⓣ	TRAILHEAD
Ⓟ	PARKING
→	DIRECTION OF HIKE
△ (with tent)	CAMPGROUND
⚏ (picnic)	PICNIC SITE
o━━	CLOSED GATE - NO MOTOR VEHICLES
) (	BRIDGE
···∼··∼	RIVER OR STREAM
⋎⋎⋎	MARSH
△	VIEWPOINT OR PEAK
⊟	BENCH
+++++	RAILROAD TRACKS
▬ ▬ ▬	PARK BOUNDARY
→•—	HIKER'S STILE

ACKNOWLEDGMENTS

Although I did all the writing for this guide, my nine-year old son, Kevin, is listed as coauthor, and for a very good reason. Without his interest in hiking and nature, it may very well have never been written. As a companion on the trail, and as a constant push at home (especially when he attempted to compute what his share of the income from the book would be), Kevin has played an important role from start to finish.

My wife, Mary, also deserves mention; she has been a trail companion for more than twenty years, even though she prefers what she describes as "Midwest walks" where there are few hills, which sometimes conflicts with my desire to reach the highest spot around. Her suggestions on what to include in the trail entries were taken seriously.

Finally, I wish to thank the people at The Mountaineers for giving me the opportunity to share some of my favorite hikes with others.

Hikes Within 20 Miles of Downtown Sacramento

Many trails near Sacramento are paved for year-round use.

1. Discovery Park Nature Trail Loop

Type:	Dayhike
Difficulty:	Moderate for children
Distance:	2 miles, loop
Hiking time:	2 hours
Elevation gain:	None
Hikable:	Year-round
Map:	Sacramento County Parks and Recreation

Discovery Park is the western terminus of the American River Parkway. This large park has swimming, boat launching, picnicking, hiking, and two archery ranges (one a target range and the other a

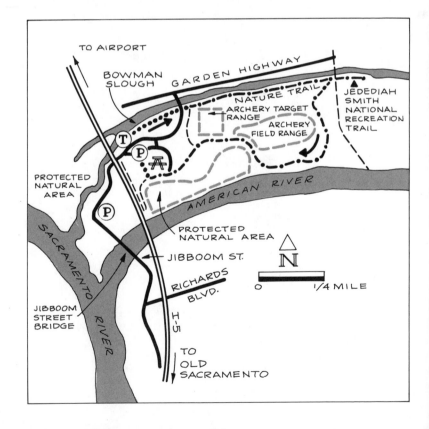

field archery range). It sits at the confluence of the American and Sacramento rivers not far from Old Sacramento, and is bounded on the north by Bowman Slough. Several large areas of natural riparian growth have been protected as nature preserves.

Take the Richards Boulevard exit off I-5, head west to Jibboom Street, and take the Jibboom Street Bridge north over the American River. Continue to the end of Jibboom Street, enter the park, and turn right to head back under the freeway. About 200 yards past the freeway you come to an overflow parking area on the left side of the road. Either park there or across the road in the regular parking lot.

The nature trail begins at the northeast corner of the overflow parking area, and follows the Jedediah Smith National Recreation Trail along the banks of Bowman Slough. Luxurious riparian growth, including large wild grape vines, covers the bank of the slough, and at 0.25 mile the pedestrian and bike trails join as they pass underneath a bridge. Have the children look for nesting pigeons and swallows here. In the wild, pigeons nest on rocky cliffs, but in urban areas they use bridge structures as well as ledges of tall buildings. The paved trail follows along the slough, with occasional trail spurs leading down to non-maintained dirt trails nearer the water.

At 0.5 mile there is a large open field to the right that can be seen through openings in the willows. The trail here has a closed, quiet feeling, and it is easy to have the children imagine they are far from civilization. Leave the paved trail and head down to the dirt trail nearer the slough and have them pretend they are the first people to explore the region. They should keep an eye out for various birds and wildlife, as well as look for edible fruits (blackberries, elderberries, and wild grapes all grow along this section).

The pedestrian trail merges with the bike trail at 0.75 mile. Take a right here to head back toward the parking lot. You pass through an endangered species protection area, and at just under 1 mile you come to a drainage area with a thick growth of trees. Part of the field archery range is on the right, and you should caution the children about leaving this section of the trail. Caution signs have been posted along here.

As you pass through the grove of trees there is a large open field where plenty of birds can be observed during the spring, and where children can look for various wildflowers. They can find a wide variety of blooms or seeds during most of the year.

Just past 1 mile the trail passes near a section of the levee that keeps the American River from overflowing into the park during the winter and spring. You can climb to the top of the levee to overlook the river, which is controlled by levees and is little more than a large channel along this section. Access to the riverbank is limited, but there are some non-maintained trails down to the water.

If you or your children head down to the water's edge, remember

Some people prefer to take the easy way down the river.

that the river is flowing swiftly through the channel here, and is not safe to wade or swim in.

By 1.25 miles there are large patches of blackberries along the trail, and the children can pick the berries as they ripen in the summer. The field archery range comes into view on the north side of the trail just past the blackberry patches, and by 1.5 miles there are large vines of wild grapes hanging from the trees along the trail. These tart grapes can be picked during the fall as they ripen.

The field archery range is on the north side of the trail just past 1.5 miles, and there is a small playground near the bike trail that leads off to the right after the archery range. You can return to the parking lot by taking a right here, or you can continue straight on the hiking trail.

At 1.75 miles, just before the trail goes under the freeway, there is an information kiosk on the north side. The plaques here have information about the human and natural history of the region, which may be of interest to the children.

You leave the trail at the kiosk, and cross the large picnic area to return to the parking area at 2 miles. You can have lunch here as the children play on the play apparatus.

2. Miller Park Levee Trail

Type: Dayhike
Difficulty: Easy for children
Distance: 1.5 miles, loop
Hiking time: 1 hour
Elevation gain: None
Hikable: Year-round
Map: Sacramento City Parks and Recreation

Miller Park is operated by the City of Sacramento, and is the location of the city marina. Large pleasure boats, primarily power, are berthed here beneath covered docks, and children like to look at the boats and talk about what they are used for and what it would be like to own one. The park itself is a small peninsula that is surrounded by the Sacramento River on the west and the marina on the east.

Head to the west end of Broadway in downtown Sacramento, and follow the signs to Miller Park. Drive to the south end of the parking lot and park in the turnaround area.

From the parking area, walk out to the end of the peninsula, where you can look over the entrance to the marina. Large boats are frequently seen entering or leaving the marina.

To begin the hike, turn right and head north along the banks of the river. There is no swimming or fishing along the river here, and

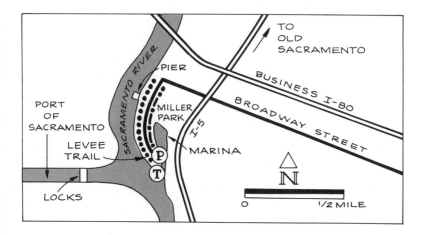

There is a long history of boating on California rivers.

there is little access to the edge of the water.

Across the river from Miller Park you can see the locks that hold the water in the turning basin at the Port of Sacramento. Large ships come into the turning basin via the Sacramento River Deep Water Ship Channel.

For the first 0.25 mile there are willow and cottonwood trees growing along the steep bank of the river, and just past 0.25 mile the side of the levee is clear of growth and covered with large rocks.

The park rules do not allow swimming or wading because the river flows quite powerfully along this straight stretch, but you can walk down to the water's edge with your children to skip rocks or throw sticks into the main channel to watch how fast they float away.

By 0.5 mile there are several paddle-wheelers and an old ferry boat visible on the other side of the river. Just before 0.5 mile there is a fishing pier that juts out into the river, and the boats are in full view across the river. The children like to walk out to the end of the pier and watch sticks and leaves float by on the fast-moving water.

The trail dead ends among more large cottonwoods at about 0.75 mile. At that point, take a right turn and cross over the road that leads into the park to the paved path that runs above the marina.

Follow this path as it leads back to the end of the park. During this stretch the children can look at the wide variety of boats in their covered berths, and talk about what each type of boat is used for. There are water-ski boats, large and small cabin cruisers, bass-fishing boats, and other types of boats berthed here, and there are several observation decks near the paved path that overlook the marina, where you can stop and have a snack while looking at the boats.

The hike ends at about 1.5 miles at the turnaround. You can have a picnic lunch on the levee overlooking either the river or the marina.

3. Goethe Arboretum Loop

Type: Dayhike
Difficulty: Easy for children
Distance: 0.5 mile, loop
Hiking time: 45 minutes
Elevation gain: None
Hikable: Year-round
Map: None

The Goethe Arboretum on the California State University campus has paved paths leading through groves of native and exotic trees that grow in Northern California. On the south end of the arboretum there

This old redwood lived through many human eras.

is a native plant section that includes native flowers and shrubs in addition to trees. This hike is a good introduction to the plants that may be encountered along the trails in this guide. It is also a good hike to take on an afternoon when you don't want to do a lot of walking, but just want to take a pleasant stroll.

Take the front entrance to the campus off J Street at Carlson Drive. The arboretum is on your right. Parking is restricted on campus, and you must park in spaces reserved for visitors except on Sundays. Take a right turn and head toward the student health center for the nearest parking.

The hike through the arboretum can be free-form, but a right turn on the path as you enter takes you on a generally curving loop around the outside of the trees. Have the children guess whether trees are native or exotic (brought to the region by humans), and then identify them by the plaques that are found at the base of each tree.

As you reach about 0.25 mile (just past a tool shed on your right) a path heads straight toward some maintenance buildings as another curves back into the trees. Take the path straight ahead, which leads to the native plant section of the arboretum. Have the children read about the plants here, because they are likely to find them on other hikes in the region.

After exploring the native plants, return to the trail junction, and return to the arboretum entrance. There are some picnic tables near the entrance where you can have a snack and talk about what trees you have seen.

---

4. Paradise Beach Trail Loop

Type:	Dayhike
Difficulty:	Moderate for children
Distance:	2 miles, loop
Hiking time:	2 hours
Elevation gain:	Minimal
Hikable:	Year-round
Map:	Sacramento County Parks and Recreation

Paradise Beach Recreation Area is part of the American River Parkway, and is located on a wide bend of the river near California State University. In addition to a popular summer swimming site, the

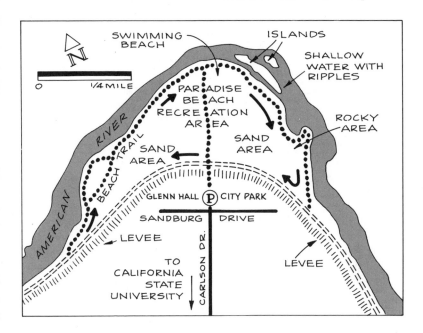

beach area includes large sand areas and thickets of riparian growth with willow, cottonwood, sycamore, and wild grapes. The river along the recreation area varies from deep, fast-flowing water on both ends of the area to shallow ripples and rapids in the center around the bend of the river. High water from past winter floods has deposited sand and gravel along the river at the bend. Plants have slowly taken over the gravel and sand areas since Folsom Dam, completed in the mid-1950s, has controlled winter floods.

Turn north on Carlson Drive off either H or J streets near the front entrance to California State University, and continue on it until it dead ends at Glenn Hall Park. You can either park in the parking lot of this small city park or along Carlson and Sandburg drives.

Paradise Beach Recreation Area is separated from Glen Hall Park by a high flood levee, and this hike turns to the left as you cross the levee and reach the bottom. Side trails cut across the sand and gravel to the beach every 100 yards or so. At about 0.25 mile, a road to the left leads to the top of the levee, but stay on the dirt trail that leads straight ahead.

The light growth of trees that has covered the sandy area to the right now turns to a thick growth of wild grapes and elderberry. Both of these are edible as they ripen, and the children like to taste these wild fruits. Explain that you only taste what you can easily identify in the wild, because some berries are poisonous.

You may also have the children guess why the plant growth has changed here. The most likely answer is that the river has begun to straighten out and never left thick deposits of sand and gravel to prevent plant growth. This gave plants in this area a head start over those in the areas you have passed.

At just under 0.5 mile, where the growth thins out as the trail nears the river, a lightly used trail heads down to the riverbank. The water flows quite rapidly here, and access is limited, so take a sharp right turn to head back upriver.

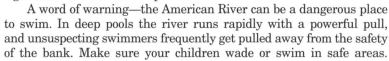 A word of warning—the American River can be a dangerous place to swim. In deep pools the river runs rapidly with a powerful pull, and unsuspecting swimmers frequently get pulled away from the safety of the bank. Make sure your children wade or swim in safe areas.

There is a good picnic spot on a point that juts out into the river after about 100 yards. The children can wade along the shore here as the trail leads out to the point.

The trail continues along the riverbank until a flat area at about 0.6 mile where the river is shallower, with some ripples, where the children can safely wade farther out.

The trail then heads inland away from the river and rejoins the primary trail. By 0.75 mile the trail leads down to the sandy beach where the walking is a little more difficult, but where the children can play in slow-moving water. By 0.8 mile you come to the main swimming beach, where the water is shallow enough that the children can play in it without you having to worry. This area is sometimes crowded during warm summer months, and you may want to continue along to about 1 mile where the water is still inviting, but the beach has narrowed enough that it is not as inviting to the casual sun-bather.

Trails lead back to the parking lot from the main beach, and you can complete a 1-mile hike by taking one of these. For a longer hike, continue on upstream along the river for another 0.5 mile or so.

The riverbank becomes less sandy and rockier along here. As high water is slowed down by the bend in the river, large rocks and gravel are deposited along the banks before the sand is, and this makes the upstream side of the bend rockier. Children like to explore among the rocks along here to find flat, smooth stones to skip across the water.

You may turn back anytime along this stretch of the trail; to make a 2-mile loop, do so at about 1.5 miles. The trail spurs lead through the riparian growth across the rock and sand banks to the levee. Turn right on the trail at the bottom of the levee, and follow it back to the trail to the parking lot at 2 miles.

This hike can be very hot during the summer months, and you should consider swimming to be a part of any summer hike. The hike is really more pleasant in the evening during the summer, and during the fall and spring when there are fewer people around and there is more birdlife to observe. The water is not so inviting during these seasons, however.

5. Del Paso Park Discovery Nature Trail

Type:	Dayhike
Difficulty:	Moderate for children
Distance:	2 miles, round trip
Hiking time:	2 hours
Elevation gain:	None
Hikable:	Year-round
Map:	Sacramento City Parks and Recreation

The Sacramento Science Center includes a natural history museum that is designed for children, and it has a number of hands-on exhibits inside. Outside, the museum has a discovery trail where children can learn about native plant communities on a short self-guided walk. The center is located at the west end of the city-owned Del Paso Park, and the short self-guided discovery hike can be extended into a longer nature hike where you may see such unusual urban creatures as roadrunners and coyotes.

Park in the Science Center parking lot off Auburn Boulevard about 0.25 mile east of Watt Avenue. From the parking lot head

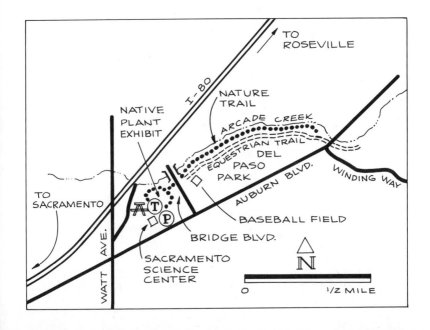

Large oak and bay trees often provide climbing opportunities along with cool shade.

toward the front entrance of the center, and the Discovery Nature Trail is to your right.

Begin the trail by going through about 0.2 mile of paved trail with plots of various native California plant communities on both sides of the trail. At about 0.2 mile the interpretive trail turns sharply to the left just before Arcade Creek. To the right is a dirt trail that heads upstream away from the Science Center. Take that trail and cross a paved road in about 200 yards.

As you cross the road you come to a baseball field on the right as the trail curves back to follow along the creek. A wider equestrian trail is located about 50 feet away from the creek, but the creekside trail is more interesting because the children can explore along the banks, look for creatures in the creek, and climb over fallen trees.

At about 0.5 mile the creekside trail joins with the equestrian trail as it crosses a large field that is full of wildflowers and birds during the spring. I saw a rare (at least for the Sacramento area) roadrunner during a summer hike here as I was writing this guide, as well as signs of coyote. I saw no traps, however, that indicated that these were the infamous Wile E. Coyote and Road Runner of television cartoon fame.

At about 0.75 mile the trail leads down to a small beach area at the creek that is often visited by great blue heron and other water birds. This is a good spot to stop for a lunch break or rest. The children can explore along the creekbanks, wade in the water, and hunt for frogs among the cattails and rushes.

After a break you can continue along the trail for another 0.25 mile until it reaches Auburn Boulevard at 1 mile. This is a good turnaround, although the trail does continue on the other side of Auburn Boulevard for some distance.

You may want to return to the Discovery Nature Trail by the trail (hiking or equestrian) you did not take on the trip out.

You rejoin the Discovery Nature Trail at about 1.75 miles, where you continue straight ahead along the creek to complete the loop. The Science Center is an excellent place to visit after you have completed the hike, and there are picnic tables behind it for those who wish to have lunch.

---

6. Arcade Creek Trail

Type: Dayhike
Difficulty: Moderate for children
Distance: 2 miles, round trip
Hiking time: 2 hours
Elevation gain: None
Hikable: Year-round
Map: Arcade Parks and Recreation Commission

This hike follows along the banks of Arcade Creek from just before Garfield Avenue to the American River College campus. The Arcade Creek Greenbelt is a narrow strip that runs between the creek and the backyards of the houses that border it, but there are large parks on both ends of the trail. Arcade Creek Park is the beginning point of the greenbelt, and the American River College campus and nature preserve are at the end.

You have two choices for beginning this hike. You can park at the parking lot of Arcade Creek Park, which is reached by turning south on Hackberry Lane off Madison Avenue, and then west on

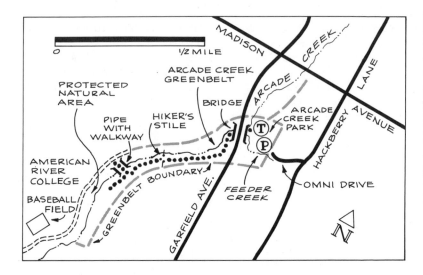

Omni Drive to the parking lot, or you can park along Garfield Avenue near where Arcade Creek passes underneath. The latter is the best choice when there is high water in the creek.

From Arcade Creek Park, head past the basketball and tennis courts and the large lawn area to the banks of Arcade Creek. Cross over a small feeder creek from the lawn area (there is no bridge here, and it is sometimes difficult to ford the creek during high water), follow the path beneath the Garfield Avenue bridge, and follow the trail as it climbs up from the creek.

CAUTION For the first 0.5 mile the trail follows along the top of the creekbank, and there are occasional spur trails that lead down to the water's edge. The water in the creek is shallow most of the year, but there is a strong current during times of high water after heavy rains in the winter. The children may want to explore along the creek when it is shallow, where they may find a number of small water insects and fish.

At about 0.3 mile you pass through a hikers' stile that keeps horses and bicycles off the upper end of the trail.

The trail crosses over the creek on a large concrete pipe at 0.5 mile. The pipe is flat on top, but it does not have railings to keep people from falling in the creek, which is about 3 feet below. Be careful here, although children seem to like the excitement of possible danger (although it is very slight).

After the trail crosses the creek it becomes a wide fire road on the American River College campus. Take a right to stay near the creek.

At about 0.6 mile the first signs noting the college nature preserve appear, and all the area between the road and the creek from here

Streamside trails are favorite sites for summer hikes.

to the end of the trail is a protected natural area. The children may explore, but remind them not to collect any items and not to damage any plants.

The trail ends at 1 mile near the college baseball field. There is easy access to the creek near the end of the trail, and this is a good spot to rest and have a picnic lunch while the children explore the creek.

Return by the same route.

7. Arden Rapids Trail

Type: Dayhike
Difficulty: Easy for children
Distance: 1.5 miles, round trip
Hiking time: 1 hour
Elevation gain: Minimal
Hikable: Year-round
Map: Sacramento County Park

C. M. Goethe Park is part of the American River Parkway that extends from Folsom Lake to Discovery Park at the confluence of the American and Sacramento rivers near Old Sacramento. It has both developed and undeveloped sections, and includes baseball fields, picnic areas, bicycle trails, equestrian trails, day and overnight group camps, river access, and a large undisturbed natural area. A pedestrian bridge connects Goethe Park with Arden Bar Park across the American River.

 From US 50, exit at Bradshaw Road and take it north to Folsom Boulevard. Turn east on Folsom Boulevard, and north on Rod Beaudry Drive to the Goethe Park main parking lot.

From the parking lot, head across the picnic area toward the pedestrian bridge that crosses the American River. Take the paved trail that comes off the bridge, and continue on it for about 200 yards. As the trail takes a sharp left back toward the picnic area, a bicycle trail continues straight ahead, and a hiking trail leads off to the right and turns left to parallel the bike trail.

Take the hiking trail as it follows along a thick stand of willow and other riparian growth until it reaches a pump house at about 0.25 mile. The hiking trail continues past the pump house, but a side trail leads off to the right through the willows toward the river. Take this trail as it takes you over the sand and gravel of a sandbar that has been formed in a bend in the river.

At about 0.5 mile you reach the edge of the river near the Arden Rapids, where the water rushes around several sandbars that have willows and grasses growing on them.

The children like to find skipping stones along the shore here, and see how far out into the river they can send them. You can also have the children toss different-size rocks high into the air above the water to see if they can hear them hit the rocky bottom of the river. Heavier rocks fall to the bottom in the swiftly flowing channel, but lighter rocks are taken downstream by the swift current before they can hit bottom.

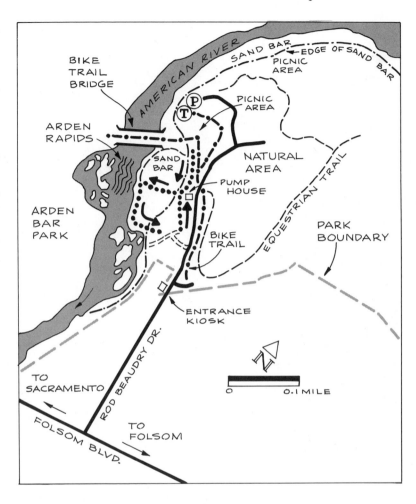

Continue the hike down the river along the sandbar until you reach a group of small islands at 0.75 mile. This is a good place to look for various birds, particularly during the spring.

To return you can retrace your route, or you can hike inland on the sandbar and bushwhack through the thickets of willow and tall weeds. This takes you through prime bird habitat, and jackrabbits often startle you as they scamper from beneath their hiding places in the undergrowth.

If you return through the thickets of willow, you reach the trail that passes by the pump house by keeping to your left. From there, return to the parking area.

For a longer hike you can take the 2-mile equestrian trail loop

Wide-open spaces are delightful on sunny winter days.

that encircles the natural area in the center of the park. This hike heads away from the river, and leads through an undisturbed forested area.

8. Ancil Hoffman County Park Discovery/Observation/Riverview History Trails Loop

Type: Dayhike
Difficulty: Moderate for children
Distance: 1.5 miles, loop
Hiking time: 2 hours
Elevation gain: Minimal
Hikable: Year-round
Map: Sacramento County Parks and Recreation

Ancil Hoffman County Park is one of many parks operated by the Sacramento County Department of Parks and Recreation within the boundaries of the American River Parkway. It is a large park with a golf course and large picnic area. In addition, it has the Effie Yeaw

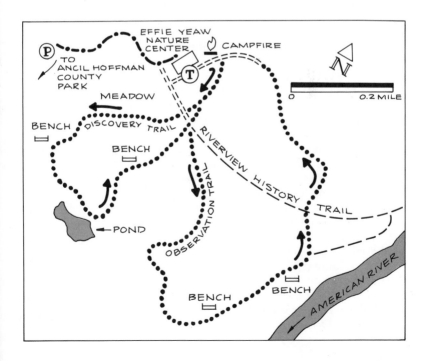

Wildlife is often seen on early-morning or late-evening hikes.

Nature Center, which includes one of the best exhibits available of the natural history of the Sacramento Valley. The nature center includes three 0.75-mile-long interpretive trails. These take you through several different plant communities where wildlife is abundant (I saw jackrabbits, deer, many small birds, squirrels, and a couple of wild turkeys the day I made the hike).

 From Fair Oaks Boulevard in downtown Carmichael, turn east on Palm Drive and follow the signs to Ancil Hoffman County Park. Park in the lot near the Effie Yeaw Nature Center.

Head for the nature center if it is open, and pick up brochures for the Observation, Discovery, and Riverview History trails. These are self-guiding trails that take you along the edge of a meadow and pond (Discovery Trail), and through riparian woodland, grassland, and oak woodland to the edge of the American River (Observation Trail). The Riverview History Trail traces the human history of the area as it leads through the riparian woodland and along the banks of the river. Each of these trails is about 0.75 mile in length.

From the rear of the nature center, take the paved trail past the campfire area to the first trail junction at about 100 yards. The Observation/Riverview History Trail heads straight, and the Discovery Trail leads off to the right. Follow the Discovery Trail as it winds south through a riparian forest.

At about 0.2 mile it crosses the fire road that is the Riverview History Trail. Just past this junction, the Discovery Trail skirts a large meadow that is home to a wide variety of birds and small mammals, and is full of wildflowers during the spring. Have the children crawl along the trail near the edge of the grass to see if they can find any small tunnels in the grass that voles and field mice have made as they venture out onto the trail to find seeds.

There are numbered posts along the Discovery Trail that correspond to the self-guiding brochure from the nature center, and several benches where you can stop and quietly observe the wildlife. Deer frequent the meadow, squirrels scamper through the oak trees, and birds flit through both.

Just before 0.5 mile, the trail curves to the left and a large pond is located on the right. This is home to many waterfowl and birds, and larger mammals come here to drink in the quiet of evening.

Have the children look for wood duck nesting boxes that have been nailed on many of the trees near the pond. For many years the wood duck population declined as their favorite nesting spots (holes in dead trees and snags) were cleared out by humans. Their numbers have increased with the aid of nesting boxes placed in live trees near feeding sites such as this pond.

The Discovery Trail winds through oak woodland as it passes the pond, and crosses the fire road/Riverview History Trail again at about 0.7 mile. Take a right on the fire road onto Riverview History Trail, and another right after about 50 feet. You will now be on the Observation Trail, which leads across a meadow and through oak woodland until just past 1 mile. There it takes a sharp left turn to parallel the American River. Although the Observation Trail is separated from the river by a rock and gravel bar, the views of the river and the distant bank are excellent. This is a good spot to look for various water birds, especially during the spring.

Between 1 and 1.25 miles there is good access to the river, and this is a good place to stop for a break. The children can wade in the water during hot days, or skip rocks out into the river when it is too cold to wade.

The Observation Trail takes a sharp left at the second junction with the Riverview History Trail at about 1.25 miles, and shortly crosses the fire road.

After crossing the fire road, the Observation Trail and Riverview History Trail follow the same route through a thick riparian forest complete with climbing grape vines that are full of purple clumps of fox grapes in the late summer and early fall. This section of the trail is a good spot for birdwatching, and is where I saw the wild turkeys during my hike.

The trail returns to the nature center at 1.5 miles.

9. Sailor Bar County Park River Trail Loop

Type: Dayhike
Difficulty: Easy for children
Distance: 1 mile, loop
Hiking time: 1 hour
Elevation gain: Minimal
Hikable: Year-round
Map: Sacramento County Park

 Sailor Bar County Park is a part of the American River Parkway, and is located on the site of a large dredging operation that was worked in the late 1800s. Mining companies used large dredges along the banks of the American River, as well as other rivers draining the foothills where gold had been mined in previous decades, to recover gold from the rock deposits that had been laid down by millennia of floods. These deposits had sufficient gold in them to make it profitable to dredge, but not to mine by hand. After the rock deposits were processed, the dredges redeposited them along the river in large piles

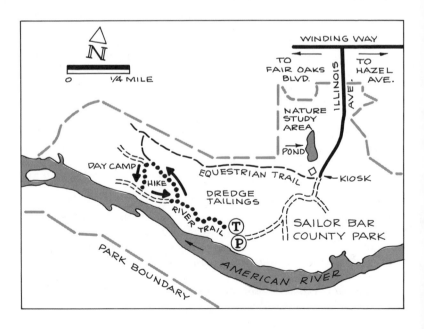

Some people prefer taking solitary walks.

called tailings. These tailings are still evident in regions where extensive dredging was done, and this hike takes you through some small examples of these.

In Orangevale, take Illinois Avenue south off Winding Way near Hazel Avenue until it enters Sailor Bar County Park. After entering the park, take a right at the first and second forks and continue to the parking lot.

The trail is a wide unpaved road as it leaves the west end of the parking lot and heads through a series of small hills, or tailings. These were mined only about 100 years ago, and all growth that you see on them has occurred since then.

During the first 0.25 mile you can take spur trails off toward the riverbanks, or you can wait until you are on your return before exploring there. Elderberries and blackberries are abundant along the trail as it winds through the tailings.

At about 0.25 mile the trail comes to another parking area that is reached from a different entrance to the park. Trails lead out of the parking area in several directions, but take the one to the right. At about 0.35 mile a trail leads off to the right and connects with the equestrian trail that encircles the park. Take this one for a 2.5-mile loop that goes toward the base of the high cliffs that overlook the river and back to the park entrance. From there you can hike to the parking area where you parked.

For the 1-mile loop described here, continue straight to the next trail junction at just under 0.5 mile, where there are signs for the day camp area. Turn left here to head through some heavy vegetation. The day camp is on your right, and several ponds are on your left. These vary in depth by season, but are generally year-round ponds that are home to numerous birds and small water animals such as frogs, fish, and turtles. The children may want to explore around the edges of these ponds, but warn them to watch for rattlesnakes, because there are a number found in the tailings.

Just past 0.5 mile the trail dead ends into a dirt road. Take a left to return toward the day camp parking area.

The trail is quite close to the river here, and you may want to explore along the banks as you continue your hike back to the car. There are rocks to skip, water animals to look for, and birds to see in the growth along the river.

The trail rejoins the unpaved road at 0.75 mile, where you return to your parking area by the same route you began on.

---

10. Phoenix Community Park Vernal Pool Trail Loop

Type:	Dayhike
Difficulty:	Easy for children
Distance:	0.5 mile, loop
Hiking time:	45 minutes
Elevation gain:	None
Hikable:	Year-round
Map:	Orangevale Parks and Recreation Commission

Vernal pools are a rare natural phenomenon that occur in few regions of the world. Northern California has more of these saucerlike depressions than any other place, and a large portion of Phoenix Community Park is a protected area where a number of these pools can be observed. Development in California has destroyed many vernal pools, and continues to threaten others, and the Orangevale Parks

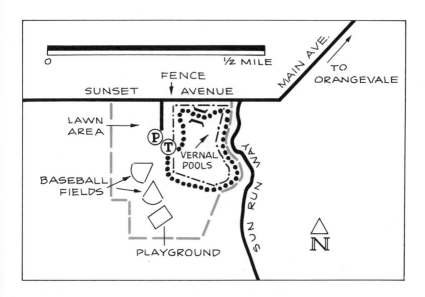

and Recreation Commission has protected sites in both Phoenix and
Orangevale community parks. The pools are found in grasslands or
in large open areas in oak woodlands where there is an impermeable
layer of soil such as clay. During winter the depressions fill with
water, which cannot seep into the soil. As a result, it slowly evaporates after the rains stop. A number of plants have adapted to this
fluctuating water level, and bloom in succession as it drops in the
spring. Concentric bands of contrasting colors then rim the pools.

Phoenix Community Park is reached by turning south on the
entrance road from the east end of Sunset Avenue in Orangevale,
across from where the old Phoenix Field Airport was located. Park
in the lot near the baseball fields.

The 0.5-mile trail enters the vernal pool area on the east side of
the parking area. The trail winds to the north past a number of pools,
which are nothing but deep depressions in the middle of an open oak
forest and grassland during the summer and fall, but are full of color
during the spring.

Have the children keep a count of how many different-colored
blossoms they can locate along this trail. Are the colors of blossoms
different at different ponds?

At about 0.2 mile the trail crosses several ponds on a footbridge,
and then follows east and then south around the park boundary. At
about 0.4 mile the trail crosses the southern end of the pools area
and continues in a westerly direction to return to the parking area
by the baseball fields.

There is a large picnic area and playground in this multipurpose park where you can have a pleasant lunch after exploring the pools.

11. Negro Bar to Mississippi Bar Trail

Type: Dayhike
Difficulty: Difficult for children
Distance: 8 miles, round trip
Hiking time: 5 hours
Elevation gain: Minimal
Hikable: Year-round
Map: State Park

The Folsom Lake State Recreation Area extends from Nimbus Dam near US 50, where the American River Parkway ends, to the Auburn Dam site on the American River, near I-80. Mississippi Bar,

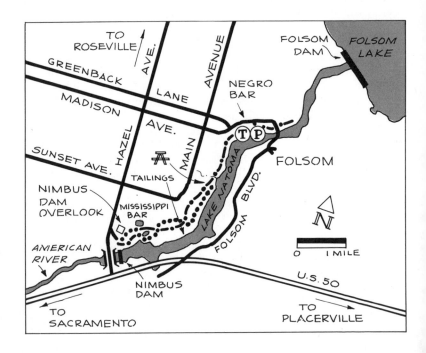

The reservoirs and lakes around Sacramento offer opportunities for a wide variety of boating.

which is located just upstream from Nimbus Dam, was a prime gold dredging area in the late 1800s, and is now the site of huge tailing piles that are crisscrossed by hiking trails. Negro Bar, 4 miles upstream from Nimbus Dam, was also a gold dredging area, but on a somewhat smaller scale, and has been a favorite swimming and boating spot for Sacramento residents since Folsom and Nimbus dams were completed in the mid-1950s. Hiking and biking trails extend along the river between the two, and provide families with an opportunity to enjoy a long hike within close driving distance of Sacramento.

From US 50, take Hazel Avenue north to Madison Avenue; turn right and continue straight as this merges with Greenback Lane. From Greenback Lane, turn right onto the Negro Bar entrance road. Enter the park and proceed to the Negro Bar Assembly Area parking lot near the swimming area. If you want to make this a 4-mile one-way hike, park one car at the Nimbus Dam Overlook near Hazel Avenue and US 50, and another at the Negro Bar Assembly Area.

Take the paved bike trail as it winds past the parking lot and turns south along the river. For the first mile the trail runs along a narrow shelf between the engineered bank of Lake Natoma and the high cliffs that overlook the lake and river area. The children can watch for boats in the lake and wildflowers on the side of the cliffs, and see if they can notice the geological formation that made this a prime gold mining region.

The eroded cliffs offer a cross-sectional view of the various deposits that were made as the Sacramento Valley filled with sediment millions of years ago, and the layers of gravel deposits interspersed among the more solid layers are the ones that contain gold ore.

At about 1.25 miles the steep cliffs aren't so close to the lakeshore, a creek comes in from the right, and the hiking trail leads off toward a small peninsula to the left. There is a picnic table just above the small pond that lies beside the trail on the creek. This is a good site to stop for a rest and a lunch. If any hikers appear tired, this is a good turnaround. Return by the same route for a 2.5-mile trip.

To continue the hike, follow the hiking trail as it leads across the paved biking trail toward the lake shore. At about 1.5 miles the trail moves inland and winds through some huge piles of tailings that were left from the gold dredging. There is a tall mountain of tailings here that stands above all the rest, and the trail winds around it.

Vegetation in this area has come back strongly, and there are some quite large stands of trees scattered throughout the tailings, particularly in depressions and level areas that hold water from the rainy season.

By 2 miles the trail levels out as it follows along some large power lines, and continues in a relatively straight line until 3 miles. This section of the trail is a good birdwatching area.

At 3 miles the hiking trail begins a series of turns that leads it back and forth across the bike trail. Just before 3.25 miles the hiking trail comes to several large inlets of the lake that are full of fish and small water animals such as frogs and turtles. Children like to explore along these as they search for the water animals and look for small birds that live in the vegetation around the edges.

After the inlets the trail crosses the bike trail once more, and passes a large pond that lies among piles of tailings at about 3.5 miles. This pond is a feeding site for water birds, and smaller birds such as redwing blackbirds are abundant among the cattails and rushes at the edge. Deer, rabbit, and coyote come here to drink in the cool of late evening.

Between 3.5 and 4 miles the hiking trail again follows the bike trail as it approaches Nimbus Dam. If you are only hiking one way, continue toward the dam and follow the trail to the overlook. If you are making the return trip, you may want to stay on the bike trail the entire return distance. This is an easier hike, and gives everyone a change of scenery.

12. Orangevale Community Park Nature Trail Loop

Type: Dayhike
Difficulty: Easy for children
Distance: 1 mile, loop
Hiking time: 1 hour
Elevation gain: None
Hikable: Year-round
Map: Orangevale Parks and Recreation Commission

Orangevale Community Park is a 75-acre park sitting amidst heavy residential development. While about 50 acres of the park are developed (including a large horse riding complex complete with show ring), about 25 acres have been left in a natural state. The area is an oak woodland with several live streams and a rare vernal pool. An improved, handicapped-accessible trail with interpretive signs is

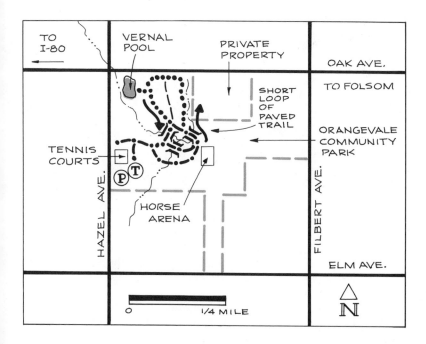

Majestic oaks are found on many hikes around Sacramento.

planned for completion sometime in 1993, but the dirt trails that crisscross the wooded area offer hikers a pleasant break from the surrounding development.

Orangevale Community Park is located in Orangevale, northeast of Sacramento. The entrance to the park is to the east of Hazel Avenue, about 0.25 mile south of Oak Avenue. Park in the lot and head north along the paved path past the tennis courts. Just to the north of the courts, take a right on the paved trail.

Stay to the right at the first fork at about 100 feet. The trail crosses a creek (which is a good site for observing birdlife) and then curves around to the left past a frisbee-golf course as it heads toward an amphitheater and horse arena.

At about 0.25 mile, just before the horse arena, take a left off the paved trail and follow a dirt trail along the creek. You can either follow a lightly used trail along the creekbank, where the children can explore for insects and other small animals, or you can take the improved trail a little farther away. During wet months, use the improved trail; the one along the creek is often wet and impassable.

Keep to the right on the trail as you continue around the perimeter of the park. A number of trails lead off to the left through the center of the park, where the children may want to explore because there is more of a feeling of wildness as you enter the middle of the forest. For a longer hike, stay to the right, though, and let the children know that they will go through the interior of the forest later.

The trail curves close to Oak Avenue at about 0.5 mile as it crosses a creek and then takes a sharp left back toward the center of the nature study area.

A spur trail leads off to the right at about 0.6 mile, and leads across the creek to a vernal pool. Vernal pools are rare, and are found in few places in the world other than Northern California. They form saucerlike depressions in grasslands where there is an impermeable layer of hard soil such as clay beneath the surface. When rains fill the depressions the water slowly evaporates. There are some plants that only live in the special environment caused by this fluctuating water level, and they tend to bloom in concentric circles as the water evaporates. Bands of contrasting colors form around the depressions as the plants bloom during the spring.

The pool you see here was once drained and many of the plants were destroyed, but local botanists are working to reestablish the original plant communities.

After you make the side trip to the pool, return to the main trail and take a right turn. You then head into the center of the forest where blue oak and interior live oak grow.

Have the children see if they can tell the difference between these two trees. (The blue oak has larger, lobed leaves and larger acorns than the interior live oak. The live oak has smaller leaves with smooth to spiny edges.)

The trail rejoins the paved trail at about 0.75 mile. Take a right, cross over the white bridge, and return to the tennis court area at 1 mile. There are picnic grounds and a play area near the tennis courts.

13. Marsh Trail Loop

Type: Dayhike
Difficulty: Easy for children
Distance: 1.25 miles, loop
Hiking time: 1 hour
Elevation gain: None
Hikable: Year-round
Map: Sacramento County Park

Gibson Ranch County Park sits along Dry Creek on the site of an old working ranch. There is a large demonstration ranch center where schools and other groups, as well as individuals, frequently come to see how the ranch operated and to observe demonstrations of such crafts as blacksmithing and horseshoeing. Barns, old farm equipment, ranch store, bunkhouse, and animal displays are also

Reeds and tule grass along waterways are excellent places to look for birds.

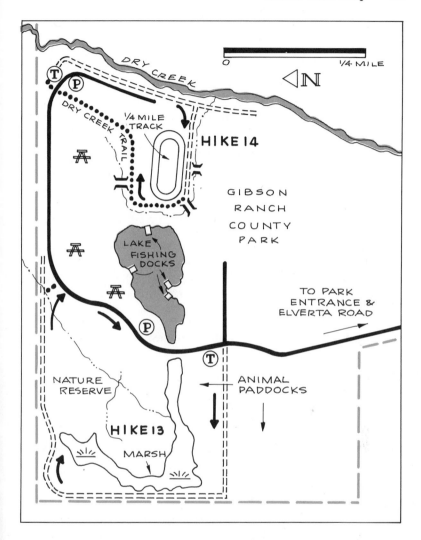

popular with visitors. In addition, there is a working horse farm with paddocks and training areas that attracts visitors. A large fishing lake with several piers lies between the farm center and the picnic and play areas. Hikers gravitate toward the marsh and nature reserve, as well as the banks of Dry Creek, to get away from the crowds.

Gibson Ranch is north of Sacramento, off I-80. Take Watt Avenue north to Elverta Road. Follow Elverta Road west past 28th Street and turn north (right) into the park. Continue past the entrance to the first parking area past the fishing lake.

From the parking lot, hike back the way you came along the road.

Go over the bridge at just under 0.2 mile and turn right onto the trail to the marsh and nature reserve. Follow this old farm road straight as it passes between two large pasture areas, where some farm animals are kept during various times of the year.

At about 0.4 mile the road dead ends into another road at the park boundary. Take a right and follow as the trail runs along a marsh. This section of the nature reserve is a prime birdwatching spot, and children like to see if they can identify what bird is making what sound, especially during nesting season when the males are establishing their territories.

Just before 0.75 mile, the marsh gives way to open grassland, which is full of wildflowers during the spring, and the trail turns to the right. It skirts the edge of the nature reserve until about 1 mile, when the main trail crosses a creek and continues straight as it approaches the park boundary. Just after the main trail crosses the creek, head right, across a small field near the overflow parking area, and cross the road to the picnic area near the fishing lake.

After the hike, children like to play around the lake, and explore among the cattails and rushes at its edge. The fishing piers are also favorite spots, where they can watch the ducks and geese.

Return to the parking area along the park road at 1.25 miles.

This hike can be combined with the next hike (see hike 14, Dry Creek Trail Loop) by veering left at the overflow parking lot instead of taking the right to return to your car, and continuing on the park road toward the Dry Creek trailhead. You can also drive from one trailhead to the other.

14. Dry Creek Trail Loop

Type: Dayhike
Difficulty: Easy for children
Distance: 1 mile, loop
Hiking time: 1 hour
Elevation gain: None
Hikable: Year-round
Map: Sacramento County Park

Other than the nature reserve, one of the few undeveloped areas of Gibson Ranch County Park is the bank along Dry Creek. This year-round creek, which becomes a roaring torrent during the heavy rains

Bridges are frequently needed on trails to cross seasonal streams.

of winter, has a number of access areas from the trail that follows along its upper banks. This short hike can be extended into a 4-mile loop if your hiking group wants a longer walk. This longer hike is especially good during the fall as the weather cools down, and the leaves of the wild grapes and sycamores are turning to add color to the woods.

Follow the directions to get to the previous hike (see hike 13, Marsh Trail Loop; map on page 65), but once inside the park, continue on the park road to the parking lot at the end of the road. Park near the entrance to the lot.

Head out of the north end of the parking lot to begin this hike. The Dry Creek Trail connects with the perimeter trail at the west bank of Dry Creek, where you take a sharp right turn to follow the creek south.

For the first 0.25 mile, the trail leads along the creek, and there are several spots where children can go down to the water's edge to explore. During the warm summer months they like to take their shoes off and wade in the water, or they can wear an old pair of shoes to protect their feet against glass and other sharp objects that may be littered on the banks and the bottom of the creekbed.

At 0.25 mile, the trail continues straight ahead along the creek, and you can continue along it to the southern park boundary for a pleasant 4-mile loop that encircles a number of horse pastures before returning past the ranch center to the Dry Creek trailhead.

On the hike described here, however, you take a right turn at 0.25 mile, and walk across the south end of the parking lot to the road that leads by a 0.25-mile race track for horse racing.

As you pass the race track there is a drainage ditch on your right that is full of a wide variety of water plants, and has many dragonflies, small birds, frogs, and small fish that live in it. Children like to explore along the edge of the ditch to look for these animals. Several bridges cross the ditch as it bends around the track.

Follow along the ditch on the manicured lawn area as it turns to the right at about 0.5 mile, and to the right again after another 200 yards. There is a thick growth of blackberries after the last turn, and a large picnic area across the ditch.

After the blackberries, at about 0.75 mile the lawn area gives way to an unkempt field that is covered with Russian thistles, which have a beautiful yellow flower during the summer, but which also have sharp, prickly thorns that are uncomfortable if you walk through them unawares.

Continue across the field to the parking area at 1 mile.

This hike can be combined with the previous hike (see hike 13, Marsh Trail Loop) by continuing straight at the race track and hiking west past the fishing lake to the trailhead on the west side of the entrance road.

---

15. Stone Lake National Wildlife Refuge Nature Trail

Type: Dayhike
Difficulty: Easy to moderate for children
Distance: Variable
Hiking time: Variable
Elevation gain: None
Hikable: Year-round
Map: USGS Bruceville Quad

Although information about this hike is limited as I write this guide, I have included it because of its great possibilities. Stone Lake Wildlife Refuge is currently administered jointly by the State of California and the Sacramento County Department of Parks and

Rivers and streams have dense growths of many types of willow.

Riparian growth has a large variety of trees that are home to wildlife.

Recreation, although it has been designated as a national wildlife refuge. No federal funding has been approved for the refuge, however, because of opposition from some local grape growers.

Plans for opening the refuge to visitors, at least on a limited basis, are being made by the state and county, and should be complete by the time this guide goes on sale.

Stone Lake National Wildlife Refuge will be an excellent hiking area for those interested in migrating birds and waterfowl, and it is close to the intersection of the Hood–Franklin Road and I-5, just south of Sacramento.

For current information on hiking at the refuge, contact the Sacramento County Department of Parks and Recreation (3711 Branch Center Road, Sacramento, CA 95827; 916-366-2066).

Hikes Within 20 to 40 Miles of Downtown Sacramento

Shaded trails can be comfortably hiked even in midday sun.

16. Consumnes River Preserve Nature Trail

Type: Dayhike
Difficulty: Moderate for children
Distance: 3 miles, round trip
Hiking time: 3 hours
Elevation gain: Minimal
Hikable: Year-round
Map: USGS Bruceville Quad

The Nature Conservancy has acquired more than 3,000 acres of land along the Consumnes River near I-5 about 25 miles south of Sacramento. The Consumnes is the largest undammed river in the Central Valley, and the winter rains frequently cause the river to overflow its banks and deposit rich silt on the lowlands of the Consumnes River Preserve. The valley oak riparian forest in the preserve is the largest and highest quality stand of streamside valley oak in the state. These riparian oak forests are among the rarest habitats in California. Riparian forests once covered more than 800,000 acres of the Central Valley, but only about 8,000 acres are left today. The 700-acre stand of valley oak found in the Consumnes River Preserve is the among the best found. Valley oak, among the largest oak found in the world, are just one of a number of rare or endangered species of plants and animals found in the preserve. Others include both lesser and greater sandhill cranes (September through April) and Swainson's hawks. More than 200 bird species have been seen in the preserve (including migratory waterfowl that come in large numbers during the fall migration), and it has one of the best marsh wildflower blooms in Northern California during spring and early summer.

Take the Twin Cities exit off I-5 about halfway between Sacramento and Stockton. Head east on Twin Cities Road to Franklin Boulevard. Turn south and continue 1.5 miles to the preserve entrance.

Begin the hike by heading through the hikers' stile, and the trail leads between an open field and a slough ringed by willows, reeds, and rushes. Have the children watch and listen for different birds along here. Redwing blackbirds are particularly numerous along the shores of the slough.

By 0.25 mile a canopy of oak and cottonwood covers the trail as

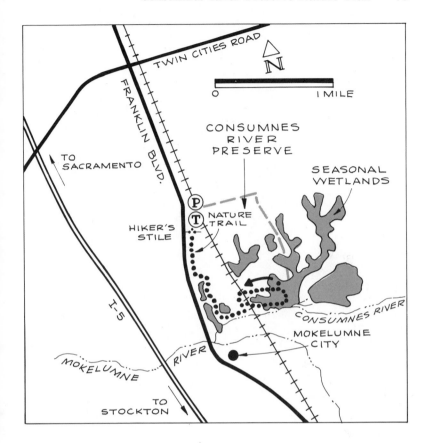

it crosses a floodplain. Several wooden footbridges keep the trail above the wettest areas along this section.

The trail leaves the forest canopy by 0.3 mile and passes by a seasonal wetland that is being restored by Ducks Unlimited. It soon rises above the wetlands on a small levee that separates the seasonal wetlands and a slough to the right.

Have the children listen closely for the many different bird sounds that come from the growth along the slough, and see if they can match the sounds with the birds.

The trail reenters a canopy of willow at about 0.75 mile, and the trail leads away from the slough. By 0.8 mile the trail takes a sharp turn to the right as it crosses over a larger footbridge and continues to follow the slough.

At just past 1 mile the trail curves back to the left as it nears the river. Several spur trails lead down to the river between 1 mile and the railroad tracks at 1.25 miles.

New bridges are being built on trails as more and more hikers use them during winter months.

A reminder: The current is quite strong here, and children should not try to wade or swim in the river. They can, however, use the access trails to look for large birds such as egrets and herons on the far bank.

At 1.25 miles the trail curves away from the river and crosses beneath a railroad trestle.

The trail returns to the riverbank and leads through a thicket of brambles until it opens up in an oak forest at about 1.3 miles. Have the children look for clues here that indicate how high the river floods during the winter. (Debris is found intertwined with the trees hundreds of yards away from the river and several feet above the ground.)

At about 1.5 miles the trail comes to an open space beneath the oak trees and near the river. This is an excellent place to stop for lunch and have the children explore both near the river and in the grassland beneath the scattered oaks. Large birds are frequently seen on the far bank of the river where there is thick riparian growth.

Two broad roads lead out from the open space. Take the one to the extreme left as it heads back toward the railroad tracks. At about 1.75 miles there is a sign noting that the broad expanse of grassland straight ahead is a protected area. Take a sharp left here toward the railroad tracks.

You reach the tracks at just under 2 miles, where you take a left after going under the tracks and rejoin the main trail. From here you return by the same route you came.

During the 1-mile trek back to the trailhead, you can have the children look for the different kinds of willow found in the preserve (at least four and maybe six). These can be distinguished by the shape of their leaves and how their limbs grow from their trunks. They can also see how many different kinds of birds they can spot in the oak trees along the trail.

The preserve is, as mentioned earlier, on a floodplain, and is often under water during heavy rains in the winter. You can contact the preserve manager (916-686-6982) for information on the condition of the trail, and for current information on the preserve.

17. Seven Mile Slough Trail

Type: Dayhike
Difficulty: Easy for children
Distance: 1 mile, round trip
Hiking time: 1 hour
Elevation gain: Minimal
Hikable: Year-round
Map: California State Park

The Sacramento–San Joaquin Delta, with thousands of miles of rivers, sloughs, levees, and marshes, is one of the world's outstanding water recreation areas. The region attracts boaters, swimmers, and water-skiers, but it also offers some of the best birdwatching in the

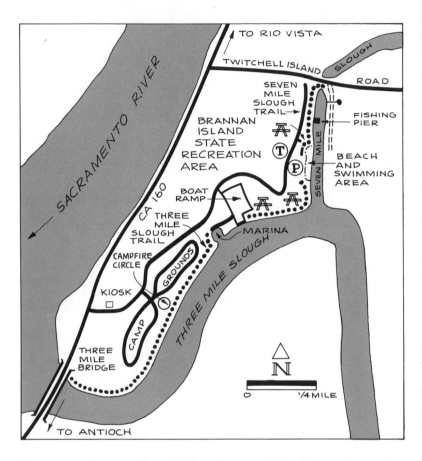

West, as well as excellent fishing. Brannan Island State Recreation Area is one of the more popular locations in the delta, and a hike along the banks of Seven Mile and Three Mile sloughs is an easy introduction to the region.

Brannan Island State Recreation Area is located southwest of Sacramento. Take I-80 west to CA-12 and head east to CA-160. Go south on CA-160 to 3 miles south of CA-12, between Rio Vista and Antioch. Turn east off CA-160 into the recreation area, and continue past the entrance kiosk, campgrounds, and boat ramps to the parking area near the swimming area on Seven Mile Slough.

For a 1-mile hike, head north along the banks of Seven Mile Slough. There is a paved bike path that leads out of the parking area. After the paved path turns inland near the rest rooms, continue straight ahead on a trail through the picnic area along the slough. The trail is not well-defined here, but you can hike along the banks, and the children can climb down to the water's edge at several spots in the

Hikers frequently pass by more sedentary types along rivers and streams.

first 0.25 mile. There they can watch for fish, turtles, and other water animals, both large and small.

Water birds are plentiful here during the fall migrations, and small birds nest in the tules, cattails, and willows during the spring. At least ten species of raptors can be seen in the area throughout the year.

At about 0.25 mile a fishing pier leads out into the slough. You can walk out to the end to search the shallow, algae-clouded water for fish and other water animals.

Past the pier the thick vegetation pushes you away from the water and you come to the end of the park road at just under 0.4 mile. At the turnaround, stay to your right and follow the path as it leads to Twitchell Island Road.

Continue to circle the end of the slough to the opposite side. Along here you can see where the water is pumped through large conduits under the road. Talk to your children about how this area was once a huge marsh, and how early settlers built levees to contain and channel the water of the sloughs and creeks, and claimed the land for farming. Explain that without constant management of the levees, the water would reclaim the "islands" that were formed by the levees, and return the region to natural marshlands.

Over the years many of these "islands" that were once swamp have actually dropped far below the normal water level of the rivers and sloughs, and some are even below the bottom of the rivers. This has occurred because normal sedimentary action has filled the river channels, and the levees have been built higher to accommodate the rising rivers.

From the No Trespassing sign at about 0.5 mile, you can look down Seven Mile Slough to where it joins Three Mile Slough.

Return to the swimming area by the same route.

There is no boating allowed in Seven Mile Slough, and children like to swim at the end of the hike during warm weather.

For a longer hike, you may wish to head to the south along Seven Mile Slough to Three Mile Slough, and follow the banks of the levee as it rises high above the water. This hike is easy because it alternately follows along paved paths and unmarked trails, and you can hike as much as 3 miles one way to CA-160, where Three Mile Slough joins with the Sacramento River. This hike is best taken during the fall when fishermen are on the slough and river and migrating birds can be seen in the water and fields.

18. Riverview Trail

Type: Dayhike
Difficulty: Easy for children
Distance: 1.5 miles, loop
Hiking time: 2 hours
Elevation gain: Minimal
Hikable: Year-round
Map: East Bay Municipal Utility District

Lake Camanche now covers the site of an old gold rush town that was named after the Comanche Indians, but whose spelling was changed through a post office error. The lake, which covers part of three counties (Amador, Calaveras, and San Joaquin), was built by the East Bay Municipal Utility District (EBMUD) between 1962 and

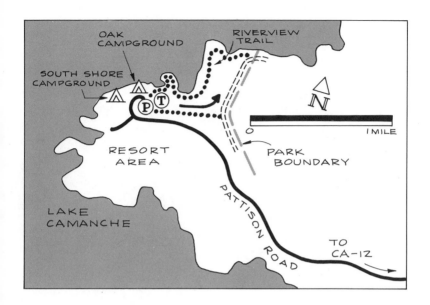

1964 as part of the East Bay's water supply system and is defined by a main earth-filled dam, spillway, and six side dikes. There has been extensive development of the recreation areas around the 53-mile shoreline of the 12-square-mile lake, and a concessionaire operates the facilities under the direction of EBMUD. Although there are no defined and maintained trails around the lake at present, there are plans for several to be built during the extensive renovation of the facilities that EBMUD began in 1989. Campers and fishermen have developed their own series of lakeside trails, however, and these offer families good access to year-round hikes at both the north and south shore facilities.

From I-5 south of Sacramento, take the Lodi exit and head east on CA-12 to Camanche Parkway South. Turn left onto Camanche Parkway South and continue to Pattison Road. Take another left and continue to the campground entrance. Follow the signs in the park to the Riverview Campground resort at the south shore of the lake. Park near the rest rooms in the campground, and walk out the east end of the campground toward the lake.

Stay on the lightly used trail uphill from the reservoir that leads along the contour of the hill through open grassland. Oak, digger pine, and manzanita grow on the hill above the trail and during the spring the hillsides are covered with a wide variety of wildflowers.

At about 0.1 mile there is a large rock outcropping beside the trail. The rocks are sandstone and you can see how the wind and water has eroded the face of the soft rocks. Children like to climb

The water levels of reservoirs can fluctuate many feet between wet and dry seasons.

around on outcroppings such as this, but remind them that rattle-snakes are common in this area, and that the sandstone is likely to crumble under a load on the steep faces of the rocks.

To avoid rattlesnakes, you should never put your hands in any area that you cannot see, and always look before you step over logs or stones.

Just before 0.25 mile the trail forks. Take the left, which continues to follow the contour of the hills above the lake. By 0.5 mile the trail dead ends into a fire road. The fire road runs along the park boundary.

Take a left on the fire road and follow it as it continues around the contour of the hills above the lake.

The fire road comes to a gate and fence at 0.9 mile. This is the park boundary, and hikers must not cross over the fence.

Take a left here and follow the fence down toward the lake. During wet years the water comes up quite high here, but after several dry years it is far below a steep cliff. Don't try to climb down these cliffs; they are unsafe. You can reach the water's edge farther along the trail.

The trail leads around several inlets of the lake, and just past 1 mile you pass the last inlet on the arm of the lake you have been circling. At this point the trail heads toward the hillside, and then takes a left turn at about 1.1 miles. After about 100 yards the trail comes to the edge of another arm of the lake. Take a left, following as the trail leads around the arm and heads back toward the campground.

By 1.25 miles you have curved around the end of the arm, and headed toward the main part of the lake.

In wet years this inlet is connected to the main body of the lake, but in dry years it is separated, and forms a small pond at about 1.25 miles. Where the pond is separated from the lake, children can climb down to the edge of the water to look for fish and small aquatic animals. The water in the pond is not suited for wading or swimming, and while the water on the opposite side of the divide is excellent for both, neither is allowed in the reservoir, because its water is used for drinking water by residents of the East Bay.

After exploring the water in the pond and/or lake, you can head back to the main trail. Use the large rock outcropping mentioned earlier as your guide. The trail returns to the campground at 1.5 miles.

For a longer hike, begin your hike at the Oak Campground, which you pass on the way to the Riverview Campground. From the lakeside of the Oak Campground, a trail heads down to the edge of the water, and if you follow this, you will connect with the trail from the Riverview Campground. This hike is about 3 miles round trip.

19. Pardee Lakeshore Trail

Type: Dayhike
Difficulty: Easy for children
Distance: 2 miles, round trip
Hiking time: 2 hour
Elevation gain: 100 feet
Hikable: Year-round
Map: East Bay Municipal Utility District

Pardee Reservoir is part of a series of reservoirs built by the East Bay Municipal Utility District in the foothills of the Sierra Nevada to supply water to homes and businesses many miles away in the East Bay. While not as large as Camanche Reservoir downstream on

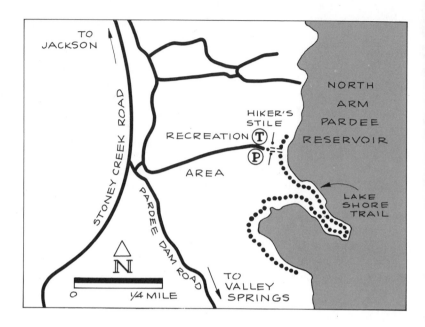

the Mokelumne River, Pardee has long been noted for its excellent fishing and resortlike camping. Formal hiking trails have never been developed around the lake, but anglers continually clear a trail around the perimeter of the lake as they tramp along searching for good fishing spots. The hillsides above the lake are covered with a scattering of oak and a thick cover of chaparral in places, but open grassland predominates along the shore. This is a good place to hike during cool winter days when the sun is hovering above the horizon, and during the spring when the hills are covered by an emerald carpet of wild grasses dotted with many bright wildflowers.

Take CA-99 south to CA-104 east to Ione. From CA-88 in Ione, head southwest on Buena Vista Road; turn left on Stoney Creek Road and then follow the signs to Pardee Dam on Pardee Dam Road. The entrance to this recreational area around the lake is near the junction of Pardee Dam and Stoney Creek roads. Enter the recreation area, turn right, and continue through the campground to the Woodpile parking lot.

From the rear of the parking lot, head through the hikers' stile and take the marked trail toward the shoreline. After about 0.1 mile you reach the shoreline, where unmarked fishermen trails lead off in both directions. Take the one to the right and follow as it leads out to the end of a small peninsula that juts out into the reservoir.

A large outcropping of rock is exposed during times of low water near where the trail from the parking lot ends. Have the children look at the large flat slabs of shale that stand upright, and have them try

Some hikes pass by geological oddities such as these upthrust sedimentary rocks.

to figure out how they were formed. Explain to them that the layers of rock were formed as sediment dropped to the bottom of a large inland sea millions of years ago, and that they once lay flat instead of standing upright as they now do. Earth movements, called uplifts, in the region caused the layers to eventually move to their current position.

The hike goes around the shore of the lake through open grass-land. Chaparral and scattered oak trees grow uphill from the lake, and if your children wish to explore, be sure to warn them to be careful of poison oak and rattlesnakes, both of which are native to the area.

The children can use some of the smaller flakes of shale as skipping rocks, but have them keep an eye out for fishermen, who don't appreciate it when their efforts are interrupted by flying rocks.

At about 0.2 mile the trail circles a small inlet that has a gentle enough slope that children can reach the water's edge easily, but caution them about swimming or wading, both of which are prohibited because the lake supplies water to homes and businesses in the East Bay region.

Although you can hike for miles along the shore of the lake, a 1-mile hike takes you out to the end of a large peninsula that juts out into the lake, and from here you have excellent views of the far shore and the hills beyond.

This is a good place to picnic and bask in the sun on warm winter days. The trail is in the open its whole length, and hot summer days can become extremely uncomfortable, particularly since you are not allowed to swim or wade in the water. Fall and spring, in addition to winter, are good hiking times because wildflowers and birds are more plentiful than in the summer.

Return to the parking lot by the same route as you came.

---

20. Western States Trail: Granite Bay to Beals Point

Type: Dayhike
Difficulty: Moderate for children
Distance: 3 miles, round trip
Hiking time: 3 hours
Elevation gain: Minimal
Hikable: Year-round
Map: Folsom Lake State Recreation Area

Granite Bay is one of the most popular swimming and boat launching areas in the Folsom Lake State Recreation Area, and is extremely crowded during peak summer weekends. The Western States

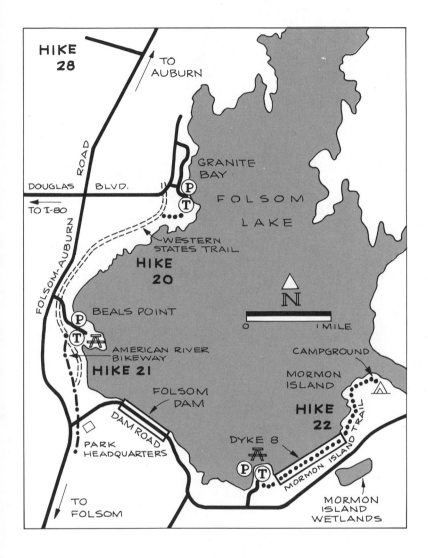

HIKE 28

TO AUBURN

ROAD

GRANITE BAY

DOUGLAS BLVD.

TO I-80

FOLSOM-AUBURN

FOLSOM LAKE

P

T

WESTERN STATES TRAIL

HIKE 20

N

0   1 MILE

BEALS POINT

P

T

AMERICAN RIVER BIKEWAY

HIKE 21

CAMPGROUND

MORMON ISLAND

HIKE 22

FOLSOM DAM

DAM ROAD

PARK HEADQUARTERS

DYKE 8

P

T

MORMON ISLAND TRAIL

TO FOLSOM

MORMON ISLAND WETLANDS

Trail, a 100-mile-long section of a pioneer trail that once extended across California and Nevada to Utah and is now a popular equestrian trail, follows the north shore of Folsom Lake, however, and offers hikers an opportunity to escape from the crowds at Granite Bay and Beals Point. Even on busy weekends when both beaches and picnic areas at the above two are packed with people, the trail is often empty of hikers. This gives families a place to hike in relative solitude without going too far from civilization.

From I-80, take Douglas Boulevard and continue east until you come to the park entrance at Granite Bay. Take the first road to the

Trails in the foothills often go through chaparral-covered areas.

right after the entrance, and stay to the right at several other forks until you reach the southernmost launching area at Granite Bay. A trail spur leads south from the launching area.

The narrow trail leads uphill through an oak forest. At about 0.2 mile the trail begins a sharp climb for about 100 feet and ends at the fire road that is the main trail. Take a left on the Western States Trail and follow as it heads along the contour of the hill above the lake. The distance to the water varies during wet and dry seasons, but at all times the trail offers outstanding views over the lake to the far shore.

Several types of oak, chaparral, and California buckeye all grow on the steep hillsides above and below the trail. Have the children look closely at the buckeye. This tree is unusual in several aspects. A remnant from times when the climate was more tropical in this region, it has adapted to the dry climate of Northern California by beginning its dormancy early in the summer and continuing it until early January, when its bright green leaves erupt, to be followed by large clumps of white flowers.

These flowers in turn give way to green seed pods that cover the largest tree seed in North America. By early fall, the seeds have shed their outer cover and become a hard, shiny, brown seed the size of a small child's fist. Children like to play with these and feel their texture. Buckeyes, with their gray-white bark, are abundant along this trail.

From 0.5 mile to the end of the hike at Beals Point, open stretches alternate with shaded sections as the trail curves in and out while following the contour of the lake with its many small inlets and peninsulas. Every 0.1 mile or so the trail comes out to the end of one of these peninsulas, and each offers a delightful picnic or rest stop. During high water the children can play along the water's edge while looking for water creatures or skipping rocks, and during low water they can hike down to the exposed rocks and soil at the tip of the peninsulas.

By 1.5 miles you reach the developed area at Beals Point where there are picnic tables and a swimming beach. During hot weather you may want to take a good rest here while the children swim, and in cooler weather it is a good spot to look out over the main dam site as you eat and rest.

Return by the same route.

21. American River Bikeway: Beals Point to Park Headquarters

Type:	Dayhike
Difficulty:	Easy for children
Distance:	2 miles, round trip
Hiking time:	2 hours
Elevation gain:	Minimal
Hikable:	Year-round
Map:	Folsom Lake State Recreation Area

The American River Bikeway extends for more than 30 miles from Beals Point along Folsom Lake to Discovery Park at the confluence of the American and Sacramento rivers in downtown Sacramento. The

Regional parks offer a wide variety of activities in addition to hiking.

bikeway follows the American River the whole distance, and is paved for year-round biking. Hikers also use the bikeway for long and short hikes, especially during the wet winter months when other trails may be too muddy to hike. The first mile of the trail follows along an earth wing dam of the mammoth, concrete Folsom Dam for about 0.5 mile and then between the dam and Folsom–Auburn Road until it crosses under Dam Road near the park headquarters.

From Greenback Lane in Folsom, take the Folsom–Auburn Road 1 mile north. Turn right at the Beals Point Picnic Area entrance. Park in the picnic area parking lot. (See map on page 85.)

Head west from the picnic area to the bike trail, where you have three route choices. You can hike along the top of the wing dam for about 0.5 mile before you have to descend to the trails, you can hike along the dirt trail at the base of the wing dam for about 0.5 mile before meeting the bike trail, or you can follow the paved bike trail the entire hike.

A hike along the top of the wing dam gives you wonderful vistas of the lake and the eastern shores, and the children like to watch for boats (at least when there is enough water in the lake for boats to sail and motor). To the west you overlook a small riparian forest that is full of active birds year-round, but is especially so in the spring nesting season.

As you approach 0.5 mile, you see a chain link fence that keeps hikers out of the spillway area. Carefully climb down the face of the wing dam to the trails below.

The final 0.5 mile of the hike takes you between the buildings below the main dam and the Folsom–Auburn Road.

At 1 mile you come to the park headquarters, where you can look over some exhibits and get information about the rest of the trails and campgrounds in the Folsom Lake State Recreation Area.

You can return by the same route you came, but children like to vary the trail. Both the dirt trail at the base of the wing dam and the paved bike trail offer you a closeup view of the riparian forest and its many inhabitants. Have the children see if they can identify any of the trees and shrubs they pass. These include various oak and willow, poison oak, ceanothus, and other chaparral plants.

22. Dyke 8 to Mormon Island Trail

Type: Overnight
Difficulty: Moderate for children
Distance: 4 miles, round trip
Hiking time: 3 hours
Elevation gain: Minimal
Hikable: Year-round
Map: Folsom Lake State Recreation Area

Folsom Lake State Recreation Area features a 18,000-acre lake, almost as much land, and 80 miles of hiking trails. The lake was created in 1955 by the large concrete dam with earth wing dams and dykes that total about 9 miles in length. The 75 miles of shoreline along the lake extend about 15 miles up the North Fork of the American River and about 10 miles up the South Fork. While fishing and swimming are the most popular activities in the recreation area, hiking and camping are also very popular. Rattlesnakes, raccoons, skunks, jackrabbits, deer, opossum, coyotes, and bobcats are some of the animals that you will either see or see signs of as you hike around the recreation area, and raptors such as kestrels, turkey vultures, and red-tailed hawks soar overhead. I saw what was either an immature bald eagle or a golden eagle land on the shore of the lake the day I was hiking this trail. Wild turkeys and quail often startle as you disturb them along the trails.

From US 50, take Folsom Boulevard north to East Natoma Street. Continue north on East Natoma Street to Dam Road. (See map on page 85.) Turn right on Dam Road and continue to the park entrance at Dyke 8. Register with the rangers as an overnight camper, and park at the rear parking lot near the picnic area.

This is an unmarked and unmaintained trail, but one that is easy to follow. From the parking area, head around the contour of the shoreline east toward Dyke 8. At about 0.25 mile you come to the end of the dyke, where you climb to the top. The dyke is almost exactly 1 mile long, and it is an easy hike along the smooth top.

From this high point, you can look out over the lake to your left, and to the right you can look over the protected Mormon Island Wetlands. This area is home to many birds and small mammals, and during the migration and nesting seasons you can catch a glimpse of many different large birds. Binoculars are very useful if you are interested in identifying the birds, and children like to use them as they hike along.

By 1.25 miles you leave the top of the dyke. Continue to follow the contour of the shoreline as it winds its way around the tip of what is known as Mormon Island. This small hillock stood above the American River and one of its tributaries, Brown's Ravine, and was the site of a Mormon settlement during the gold rush.

The hill itself is covered with a fairly dense growth of a variety of oak, and the children may want to explore the edge of the forest

as you continue around the shore to the environmental campground. Have them keep an eye out for poison oak and rattlesnakes.

By 1.5 miles the lake forms a small inlet and the land juts out into the lake some distance before curving around so you can see the much larger inlet at the mouth of Brown's Ravine. From here until you reach the camp at 2 miles, you overlook the largest marina on the lake, where weekend boaters keep their large and small sail and motor boats. The children like to watch the boats enter and leave the marina, and often follow their progress far out into the lake.

You come to a small environmental campground at 2 miles. There are a chemical toilet, a picnic table, and tent spaces here, but no water. You should talk to the rangers about campfires and stoves when you make reservations for the campsite. The area is extremely dry and has a very high fire danger in the summer and fall, and regulations about campfires vary by season. You must bring all your own drinking and cooking water, although water from the lake may be used for dishwashing if it is properly boiled.

Return by the same route, or you may want to bushwhack through the oaks as you cross the peninsula on the way back to the dyke.

Look for the many types of flowering plants found along the trails.

This is an easy introduction to backpacking for families with children because it is close to Sacramento, requires minimal climbing, and is close to water, where the children can fish and swim.

Reservations are required for all environmental campsites within the Folsom Lake State Recreation Area. Call the recreation area (916-988-0205) for reservation information for this and other environmental campsites. Because many boaters use the environmental campsites, you will have more luck reserving them during the off-season for boaters. This happens to be in the fall, winter, and early spring when hikers are more likely to enjoy the campsites.

23. Old Salmon Falls Horse Trail

Type: Dayhike
Difficulty: Moderate for children
Distance: 1 mile, round trip
Hiking time: 2 hours
Elevation gain: 200 feet
Hikable: Year-round
Map: Folsom Lake State Recreation Area

As Folsom Lake filled behind Folsom Dam, many popular swimming and hiking sites along both the north and south forks of the American River were inundated. Several of these sites are still popular, but have changed extensively with the flooding of the region. Old Salmon Falls is one of these sites. As the lake rose, the falls disappeared, but a hiking and equestrian trail still offers access to the shore near where the falls were. Private land, complete with large homes, intermingles with Folsom Lake State Recreation Area lands along this trail, and horseback riders are encountered more often than

Many trails in the foothills cross open expanses of grasslands to reach rivers and streams.

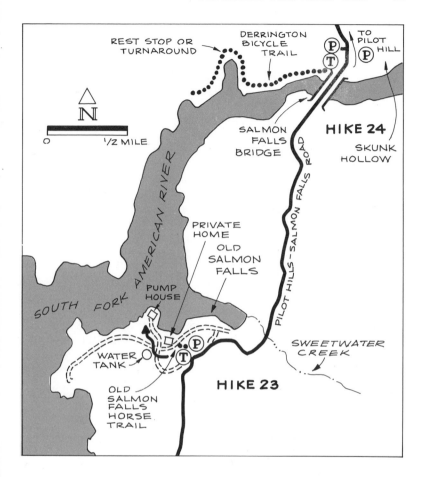

other hikers. As with other trails along the shoreline of the lake, what is accessible depends upon the water level of the lake, which fluctuates widely from season to season and year to year. After several years of drought, hikers can climb all the way down to the original course of the river, while in wet years the lake covers almost all cliffs and rocks.

From US 50, head north on El Dorado Hills Boulevard, then continue north on Pilot Hill–Salmon Falls Road and continue for just over 2 miles to the unmarked parking area at the Salmon Falls Horse Trail staging area. Park in the staging area, and begin the hike along the trail near the west end of the area.

The first 0.25 mile of the trail takes you along a level trail through oak and grassland, with some chaparral cover. Have the children see if they can identify some chaparral plants by their small trunks, hard cover, and small waxy leaves that help prevent evaporation of crucial water. At just past 0.1 mile the narrow foot trail merges with the South Side Trail. Take a left on this trail, which extends from Wild Goose Flats on the North Fork of the American River to Brown's Ravine on the south side of the lake, and offers access to almost the entire shoreline.

At about 0.25 mile, the South Side Trail crosses a maintained service road used by staff to maintain a pumping station downhill at the lakeshore. Take a right onto the service road and follow it as it curves around a large private home on the right. A large water tank is located across the trail intersection from the private home.

Just before 0.5 mile, you enter a fairly thick grove of planted ponderosa pine, which normally do not grow at this low elevation. Because the trail ends at the pump house and high-water mark of the lake at 0.5 mile, you come either to the water or, late in the season or during dry times, to the edge of the forest as the hill drops down to the water or river below.

The flat spot at the end of the road is a good picnic spot, and children like to explore along the edge of the water in both directions. Depending upon the water level, they can explore several hundred yards in either direction, and if the water is low, they can locate creeks in both directions that feed into the lake. When the water level is low, small waterfalls form on both creeks after a heavy rain.

Return to the parking area by the same route to complete a 1-mile round trip.

24. Derrington Bicycle Trail

Type: Dayhike
Difficulty: Moderate for children
Distance: 2 miles, round trip
Hiking time: 2 hours
Elevation gain: 100 feet
Hikable: Year-round
Map: Folsom Lake State Recreation Area

The Derrington Bicycle Trail was built and is maintained by mountain bike enthusiasts, and is used very heavily by mountain bikers during weekends. Cyclists are conspicuous by their absence during the week, however, and this makes this trail an ideal short hike for families any time of the year. The trailhead is located just uphill from the Skunk Hollow parking lot and the South Fork of the American River. This is a favorite raft take-out spot, and hikers can frequently watch as the rafts float down the river from above the Skunk Hollow area to the upper reaches of Folsom Lake. During high water, the lake reaches past the bridge on the Pilot Hill–Salmon Falls Road, but in dry years the original channel of the river is visible.

Follow the directions to the previous hike (see hike 23, Old Salmon

Hikers can see the high-water marks beneath this bridge, and notice the wide extremes of water levels.

Falls Horse Trail; map on page 93). Continue on the Pilot Hill–Salmon Falls Road to just north of the bridge across the South Fork of the American River. The parking lot for the trailhead is on the west side of the road. Head west along the trail. This is a bicycle trail, so beware of bikes that may come around corners at high speeds.

The trail follows the contour of the hillside about 100 feet above the river at low water, and maybe 25 feet above high water. The hillside was burned sometime in the past several decades and you can see how the first plant community to cover the hills after a major fire is chaparral. The plants included in the chaparral community are quick to sprout after a fire, because their seeds and roots are actually activated for regeneration by the heat of a forest fire. They also can tolerate the searing heat of midsummer days on the exposed hills, and help prevent erosion in subsequent winter rains. Have the children look at some of these plants and see if they can identify some of the characteristics of chaparral plants.

Views along the trail are excellent during both high and low water, and you can see how high the water gets by the marks on the bridge.

At about 0.1 mile there is a short climb and drop on the trail and the chaparral gives way to grass, where spring wildflowers are abundant. Have the children look at the red soil filled with various rocks. This is the type of soil that miners looked for when searching for gold. The various quartz rocks that can be found in the soil are frequently associated with gold deposits, and this was an area rich with deposits in the 1800s.

At about 0.25 mile there is a rock outcropping along the trail where a waterfall forms during wet winters. The children may want to climb around the rocks, but caution them about rattlesnakes, and tell how to avoid them.

Just before 0.5 mile there is a large round granite boulder jutting out of the hillside by the trail. Have the children look at how the boulder is flaking off like an onion. This is called exfoliation by geologists, and is the result of expansion and contraction of the boulder as it heats up and cools down.

After 0.5 mile there are a number of gravel bars along the river that are exposed during low water, and these were popular sites for placer mining during the gold rush.

There is no access to the water until about 1 mile because the hill is steep and covered with dense chaparral most of the way. By 1 mile the trail circles around the end of an inlet where a seasonal side stream enters the lake. This is the first access to the water, and is a good place to stop for a picnic while the children play along the edge of the lake.

The trail continues along the lakeshore for miles, and this hike can be extended as long as you want, but you can return after this stop for a 2-mile round trip.

25. Peninsula Trail to Wild Goose Flats

Type: Overnight
Difficulty: Difficult for children
Distance: 6 miles, round trip
Hiking time: 4 hours
Elevation gain: 200 feet
Hikable: Year-round
Map: Folsom Lake State Recreation Area

A long peninsula separates the north and south forks of the American River as they enter Folsom Lake. This region is very isolated, and the large campground at the tip of the peninsula can only be reached by boat or by 10 miles of curvy road from the small town of Pilot Hill on CA-49. The peninsula is formed by a long ridge that drops down quickly to the two forks of the river, and the slopes are covered by a thick growth of chaparral. As the slopes approach the lake, they have less chaparral and more open stands of oak and digger pine. The trail along the north fork of the river from the campground leads through some of the wildest and most pristine foothill areas of the Sierra Nevada. Although miners flocked to the region during the gold rush days, little trace of their invasion remains. Hikers have a real feel of wilderness as they walk along the shore of the lake here, even though they begin their hike directly across the lake from Granite Bay, the busiest and most developed section of Folsom Lake State Recreation Area.

From I-80 in Auburn, go south on CA-49 to Pilot Hill. Take Rattlesnake Bar Road from Pilot Hill for 10 miles to the Peninsula Campground. The trail begins on the north side of the campground as it heads upstream on the North Fork of the American River.

This hike is long, but relatively level, and is a good introductory overnight hike for older children. Try one of the shorter overnight hikes with younger children before you attempt this one.

You may encounter some hikers and fishermen along the first mile of the trail as it winds around many small bays and inlets. The largest of these is found at about 0.75 mile, and this is a good rest stop, where children can play around the edge of the water as they search for turtles and frogs among the reeds and rushes.

You come to another large inlet at about 1.25 miles, where you are likely to encounter either feeding or nesting waterfowl. From here to 1.75 miles, you are passing by an offshore natural preserve that includes Anderson Island. This preserve was developed primarily to protect the wild geese and other waterfowl that use the area, and you may see broods of young goslings and ducklings feeding along the shore after nesting season.

The trail continues a slow climb as you follow the curved shoreline past 2 miles, and at about 2.75 miles the trail cuts inland across a small peninsula.

At 3 miles the trail reaches the Wild Goose Flats environmental campground, which sits on a quiet inlet where the children can play along the shore as you set up camp.

If you are camping during a dry season, or after several dry years, the camp will be a considerable distance uphill from the water. In wet years the water will be quite close to the campground.

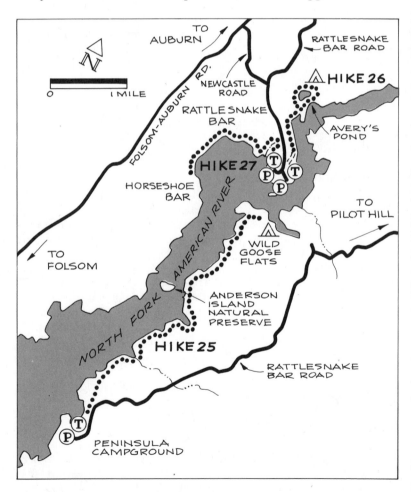

The meandering streambed of the American River is visible at the upper end of Folsom Lake during low water.

Remember that you should bring all of your drinking water for this long hike, because the water in the lake is not safe to drink without purifying.

Fall and winter are good times to take this overnight. Boaters are less likely to have reserved the campground, and the weather is not so hot as to discourage novice hikers. Call park headquarters (916-988-0205) for campground reservations and information about fire and water conditions.

Return by the same route.

26. Avery's Pond Trail

Type: Overnight
Difficulty: Easy for children
Distance: 2 miles, round trip
Hiking time: 2 hours
Elevation gain: 100 feet
Hikable: Year-round
Map: Folsom Lake State Recreation Area

As you head farther up the arms of Folsom Lake, you find fewer and fewer people, and several environmental campgrounds have been established in these far reaches of Folsom Lake State Recreation Area for the use of hikers and equestrians. The American River region is filled with history of the gold rush days, and while few buildings from that period stand today, there are occasional items that do remain. Conduits and aqueducts for water transportation were built in many parts of the gold mining region, because water was scarce away from the rivers and streams themselves. As you hike into Avery's Pond, which is itself a relic from the gold rush days, you hike by one of the large aqueducts that were built before the turn of the century. This one, as with most of those built more than a century ago, has long since deteriorated as it lost its purpose for being, and during high water in Folsom Lake, parts of it are inundated. Other sections have been washed away during high water and floods. The pond and sections of the aqueduct do remain, however, as reminders that give us a glimpse into the life of the forty-niners, as do many of the names found along the shore of the lake. Rattlesnake Bar, Horseshoe Bar, Brown's Ravine, Mormon Island, and Wild Goose Flats are all left from the colorful times when miners gave descriptive names to sites where gold was found. Many of these sites became short-lived towns and settlements, while others simply remained stopover points as the miners drifted up and down the Sierra Nevada in search of gold.

Take Newcastle Road off either I-80 or Folsom–Auburn Road (see map on page 98) and head southeast to Rattlesnake Bar Road and turn right. Continue past the entrance to the recreation area for a little over 1 mile to the end of the paved road. The road forks at the end of the pavement, and the fork to the left leads 0.5 mile to a boat launching site near the trail to Avery's Pond. Park in the paved parking lot and head back uphill on the dirt road for about 100 feet. The trail heads off to the right.

Cypress trees stand sentinel over a hillside cemetery.

This is an excellent first-time overnight hike, and the children will like to play around the edges of the pond as they look for frogs, turtles, and snakes. Large great blue herons frequent the pond, and many smaller birds come to eat the insects there.

The trail is a fire road that leads through an open meadow that is full of wildflowers during early spring before the summer heat comes.

The fire road becomes a single-track trail at about 0.2 mile as it enters an oak and chaparral zone. Have the children look at the leaves and bark of the manzanita bushes. The smooth bark covers a hard, dense wood that maintains the night's coolness long into the day, and the small, hard leaves prevent evaporation of much-needed water. During the spring the bushes have small white flowers that turn into small applelike fruits in the summer and fall. In fact, *manzanita* means "little apple" in Spanish, and both early explorers and Native Americans used the fruit to make teas and jams. It is very nutritious, and even quite tasty.

Just past 0.5 mile, the trail begins to slowly descend and passes by some large rock outcroppings on the left. The children may wish to climb on these, but there are two obstacles—poison oak and rattle-snakes. Poison oak covers the rocks, and it is impossible to climb on them without using blind handholds, which may contain snakes.

The first remains of the old aqueduct can be seen along here, and the children can look for more sections as you walk along the trail. You can discuss how these were used in pioneer days to transport water to settlements, much as we do today for the cities of Southern California.

You come to a wooden bridge with a horse watering hole at 1 mile. This bridge crosses a spring-fed swamp near Avery's Pond, and you see the pond as you cross the bridge. Take a right on a second bridge after about 50 feet, and follow the trail around the uphill side of the pond.

Caution the children about the pond; it is steep-sided and deep, and not safe for swimming or wading.

The environmental campground is located on the north end of the pond, and consists of a picnic table, a chemical toilet, and a leveled sleeping or tent site.

This camp site must be reserved. Call park headquarters (916-988-0205) for reservations. You must bring your own drinking water for this overnight, and you should check with the park officials about fires and camp stoves when you make your reservations for the campsite.

Return by the same route after spending the night.

27. Western States Trail: Rattlesnake Bar to Horseshoe Bar

Type: Dayhike
Difficulty: Moderate for children
Distance: 2.5 miles, round trip
Hiking time: 2 hours
Elevation gain: 100 feet
Hikable: Year-round
Map: Folsom Lake State Recreation Area

Gold miners often found deposits of gold along what they called "bars" of rivers and streams. These were sections of the rivers where wide turns were made around geological formations. In these turns, the water slowed down and heavier sediment such as pebbles and gold were deposited. Over centuries, these built up to large deposits of gravel, and formed the bars where the gold was found. As miners discovered deposits of gold, they identified their findings and mines by some local characteristic. The beginning and ending of this hike were both sites of finds, and Rattlesnake Bar undoubtedly got its name from the vast number of rattlers miners encountered during their digging. Horseshoe Bar got its name from the river's very definite horseshoe shape on maps. Today the Western States Trail runs along the shore between the two bars, and hikers can find solitude as they amble along the shore of the lake.

Follow directions to the previous hike (see hike 26, Avery's Pond Trail; map on page 98), but at the end of the paved road take a right at the fork instead. Continue along the dirt road for about 0.5 mile to the Pioneer Trail Staging Area. The trail leads away from the lake into the oak woods at the rear of the horse staging area.

For the first 0.25 mile, the trail leads through the woods and

Hikers frequently share the trail with horses and their riders.

comes to a creek feeding into the lake. As you cross the creek, children like to explore, looking for frogs, turtles, and other water animals.

After crossing the creek, the trail follows the contour of the hillside just above high water of the lake. During wet years you have easy access to the water, and the children can explore along its edge as you hike, but in dry years the water is some distance from the trail. If that is the case, you may want to hike over the ridges and valleys that are normally covered with water. These are free of vegetation, and hiking is easy.

There are a number of inlets to explore during the 1 mile to the far side of Horseshoe Bar, and the children will be ready for a rest stop by the time you reach the relatively level area near the water, found at 1.25 miles.

This is a good spot for having a picnic before you head back. If the water is low, you may want to change your route somewhat (use the trail instead of the barren ground below high-water level or vice versa) as you return for a 2.5-mile round trip.

28. Miner's Ravine Nature Trail

Type: Dayhike
Difficulty: Easy for children
Distance: 0.5 mile, loop
Hiking time: 1 hour
Elevation gain: Minimal
Hikable: Year-round
Map: Placer County Parks Division

Miners shoveled and sluiced the stream gravel along this creek during the 1850s. The gold deposits in the stream gravel were known as "placer gravel" and were a rich source of gold for early miners. As they moved the gravel from the streambeds and ran it through their sluice boxes, the miners left huge piles of gravel known as tailings. After the stream had been mined out, the Allen family purchased the surrounding land from the Sierra Pacific Railroad in 1863. The Miner's Ravine Nature Preserve and trail was developed by a number of public and private groups in the Granite Bay area, and now offers residents and visitors alike an opportunity to learn about the various features of a foothill stream. Many features of a stream work together and influence each other. Trees that line the banks of the stream channel

Tall trees offer shade to open trails beneath.

help hold the bank together as their roots draw water from the stream, and their shade helps fish survive in shallow waters that would otherwise get too hot during the summer months. Along the nature trail, you will learn about the things that make a stream "work," and how various people have utilized the region over the centuries. To best use the trail, contact the Placer County Parks Division (11476 C Avenue, Auburn, CA 95603; 916-889-7750) for a trail guide to the preserve.

The preserve is located alongside the old Folsom–Auburn Road just past Granite Bay on the way to Auburn (see hike 20, Western States Trail: Granite Bay to Beals Point; map on page 85). Park in the parking lot and read the information plaques before beginning the trail from the rear left corner of the lot.

The 0.5-mile trail, which veers to the right after about 100 feet, leads through riparian growth and the trail guide includes information about the flora and fauna of the area, as well as information about how floodplains form.

At about 0.25 mile, the trail comes to the creek itself, and this is a good spot for the children to play along the banks and investigate the plants that live there. They may want to sit quietly by the water to see how many small fish they can see in the shallow ponds.

The trail makes a sharp left turn and leaves the creekside as it heads through oak and digger pine to an archaeological site. Have the children talk about how they think both the Native Americans who lived in the region, and the later miners and settlers who migrated there, felt about the region, and what they wanted from it.

Return to the parking lot at 0.5 mile.

29. Tailings and Quarry Trails Loop

Type: Dayhike
Difficulty: Moderate for children
Distance: 3 miles, loop
Hiking time: 2 hours
Elevation gain: Minimal
Hikable: Year-round
Map: Placer County Parks Department

This small 25-acre park is not only an excellent example of a typical foothill–woodland plant community, but is also the historical site of a quarry that provided foundation and ornamental granite for many of the important buildings of early California. Griffith Griffith, a Welsh immigrant who had worked in quarries in both Wales and New England, first tried gold mining after he moved to California, but soon realized that granite quarrying would be more profitable. In 1864 he established the Penryn Granite Works on the site of the present Griffith Quarry Park. The quarry was operated by Griffith and his nephew until 1918, when it closed its doors for lack of a market. Newer materials such as concrete were cheaper for building, and ornamental granite became unfashionable. While the quarry was

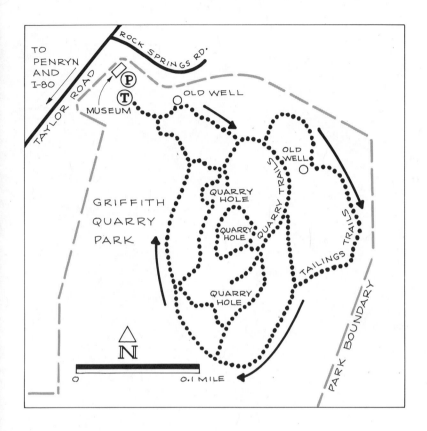

in operation, the lands surrounding the site were turned into pasture, orchards, and homesites, but the land of the quarry itself was left in an almost natural state. This left intact prime growths of the plant communities that were once typical of the entire region. Today park visitors can see large plants such as digger pines, California buckeye, and Fremont cottonwoods standing over undergrowth of toyon, coyote brush, poison oak, and a wide assortment of wildflowers, ferns, and grasses. Birds are plentiful in the park, and signs of mammals such as squirrel, rabbit, opossum, skunk, fox, and coyote can be found in the park, although the animals themselves are wary of people and seldom seen. Rattlesnakes are also found here in abundance, so be wary of them and watch where you step and reach. Large bullfrogs can sometimes be seen near the quarry holes.

Take the Penryn exit off I-80 and follow Penryn Road to Taylor Road. Turn right and follow the signs to the park near the corner of Taylor and Rock Springs roads. The trail begins at the rear of the parking lot.

Trails lead above the open quarry pits at Griffith Quarry.

There are 3 miles of trails in this small park and most people like to hike the Tailings Trail around the perimeter first to get an idea of what is contained in the park. Begin at the park kiosk and stay to your left as the trail leads through a dense growth of oak and chaparral. After about 100 feet you come to a small opening where there are the remains of an old granite-lined well that the children will like to examine.

Continue straight ahead to a larger clearing where the trail forks. Take the trail to your left as you stay in the dense vegetation. There is another old well at about 0.25 mile, and there are large piles of grout (waste rock) from the quarry holes.

The Tailings Trail continues around the park, and several spur trails lead off into the center of the quarry, where large holes are fenced off to keep visitors from entering them. The overlooks into the large quarry holes are unimpeded by the fences. These spur trails lead off at about 0.5 mile, 0.75 mile, 1 mile, and 1.5 miles.

I suggest that you complete the circuit of the outside Tailings

Trail, and then head into the center of the park on one of the Quarry Trails to explore the old quarry, after everyone has an idea of what is in the park. After the 1.5-mile perimeter hike, the rest of the hike becomes free-form as the children explore the workings of the quarry.

Caution the children against trying to climb over or go around the fences; there are very hazardous steep cliffs in the quarry area. Everyone should also be aware of poison oak and rattlesnakes, both of which are found in areas of the park.

30. Interpretive/Monument Trails Loop

Type: Dayhike
Difficulty: Moderate for children
Distance: 2 miles, loop
Hiking time: 2 hours
Elevation gain: 100 feet
Hikable: Year-round
Map: California State Park

This is as much a human history hike as it is a natural history one. Marshall Gold Discovery State Historic Park is on the site where James Marshall made his famous gold discovery in 1848. In the following year, 1849, thousands of pioneers rushed into the territory in search of riches beyond belief. And most of them found that it was impossible to fulfill their dreams of easy wealth, but stayed to make California the Golden State for the century of immigrants that followed. As most every child in California knows, Marshall made his discovery on the South Fork of the American River while building a sawmill nestled in Coloma Valley for John Sutter. The park is devoted to historical buildings and sites that commemorate Marshall's 1848 discovery.

You can reach Marshall Gold Discovery State Historical Park from either Placerville on US 50 or Auburn on I-80. The park is about halfway between the two on CA-49. Park along Main Street and begin your hike at the Sawmill Site Monument near the river.

After reading about the sawmill and gold discovery, walk toward the river for about 0.1 mile and at a T junction near the American River, turn left to go to the gold discovery site. Have the children search along the riverbanks to see what it must have been like to discover gold.

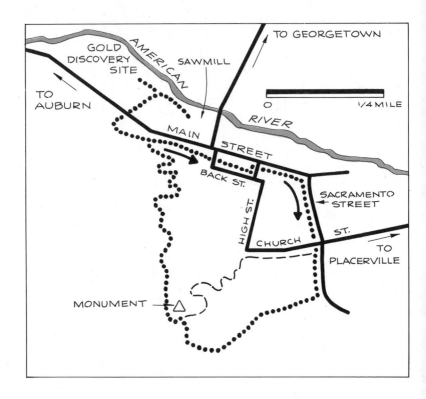

Backtrack from the site to the T junction, and continue for a little more than 0.1 mile to the replica of the sawmill that Marshall and his crew were building when they discovered gold. The children like to play around the mill and see how the old mills worked.

Return to the T junction and turn left to return to Main Street. Turn left on Main Street and head toward the center of town, where you will pass by a number of old buildings and exhibits.

At just under 1 mile take a right on Sacramento Street and head uphill. At about 1.1 miles you cross Church Street, where you can take a right to walk by two old churches (the Emmanuel Episcopal and St. John's Catholic) on an alternate route to Marshall's cabin and the James W. Marshall Monument. If you would prefer to hike a little farther uphill, continue along Sacramento Street until you come to the Vineyard House at about 1.25 miles. Take a right on the park trail just before the house, and follow it to the monument. The trail is on park property, but is bounded closely on both sides by private property until about 1.5 miles. Make sure the children stay on the trail here.

Continue on the trail until it winds up to the monument at about

1.75 miles. The children may like to take a rest here to look out over  the Coloma Valley and the American River. While you have a snack, you may want to have a conversation about the gold discovery, and how that changed the natural history of California. Suggestions to get them started might be to discuss how mining affected the rivers and streams of the area, how runoff affected rivers and the San Francisco Bay lower down, and how the general ecology of the area may have been changed.

From the monument, return to the main trail and turn right to head downhill to the parking lot at 2 miles. Many of the trees and shrubs that grow along the trail and around town are exotics (non-native plants) that were brought here by lonely miners who were homesick for familiar sites and smells.

A trail takes hikers on a walking tour of the history of the 1848 gold discovery in Coloma.

31. Ruck-A-Chucky Trail

Type: Dayhike
Difficulty: Moderate for children
Distance: 2.5 miles, round trip
Hiking time: 2 hours
Elevation gain: 100 feet
Hikable: Year-round
Map: Auburn State Recreation Area

The trails around the mountains and canyons of the Auburn State Recreation Area are often steep and tortuous, and not appropriate for families with young children or out-of-shape members. These trails lead into beautiful areas that are well worth the effort for more experienced hikers, but that are beyond the capabilities of others. Drivers Flat Road leads into the Auburn State Recreation Area's Ruck-A-Chucky Campground near the edge of the Middle Fork of the American River. Ruck-A-Chucky was an active gold mining site in the late 1800s, and got its name from the "rotten chuck" served as food in most mining camps. Through usage and slang, this became "ruck-a-chucky." The settlement near the campground became known by this term, and today is one of the most pleasant hikes along the river.

    From I-80 in Auburn, take Auburn–Foresthill Road north. Take a right onto Drivers Flat Road, heading southeast for just over 3 miles. Pass through Ruck-A-Chucky Campground to the trailhead

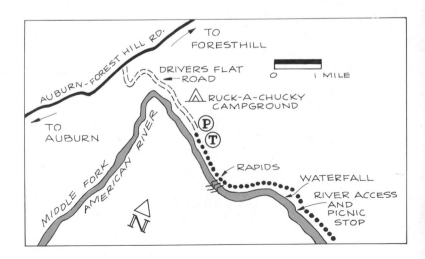

Cold rivers provide excellent swimming holes where hikers can cool off on summer days.

parking area. Drivers Flat Road is sometimes closed during the rainy season. Call the recreation area (916-885-4527 or 916-988-0205) for current information.

The trail winds along the edge of the river with gentle climbs and descents as it heads upstream. For the first mile there is little access to the river, but the children like to keep an eye on the river below to see what birds and large animals they may spot there.

During the spring this section of the trail has one of the best wildflower blooms in the foothills. The bloom begins with golden poppies (California's state flower) in late March and continues until late May when the large clusters of white blooms cover the many California buckeye along the trail.

The buckeye is a migrant from tropical climes that followed the glaciers north over thousands of years, and has had to adapt to the hot, dry summers of Northern California by leafing out in midwinter and becoming dormant by early or midsummer at the onset of wilting heat. It stays in dormancy through summer and fall until the next winter. After the blossoms fall in June the large seeds of the buckeye form inside a thick, green outer cover. These seeds, the largest of any tree in North America at about 2 inches in diameter, turn to a shiny brown by early fall. These smooth seeds are a favorite of children, who like to pick them up to feel their smooth skin and toss them downhill toward the river.

Native Americans used these seeds for food during times when acorns were scarce, as well as a way of catching fish. The seeds were slightly crushed, and floated in small ponds of rivers and streams. A substance in the seeds stupefied any fish in the pond and the natives were able to catch them by hand or net as they floated to the surface.

At about 1 mile the trail arrives at a spot high above the Ruck-A-Chucky Falls, which tumble over large boulders between sheer granite walls. Although the falls aren't accessible, children are mesmerized by the torrents of water that form hanging mists as they reach the pools at the bottom.

The trail drops down to the edge of the river at 1.25 miles, and there is an excellent picnic site where you can rest as the children explore along the riverbanks.

Return by the same route for a 2.5-mile round trip.

---

32. Old Clementine Road Trail

Type: Dayhike
Difficulty: Difficult for children
Distance: 3 miles, round trip
Hiking time: 2 hours
Elevation gain: Minimal
Hikable: Year-round
Map: Auburn State Recreation Area

In the Auburn State Recreation Area, Lake Clementine was formed when the North Fork Dam was completed in 1939 as a debris-catching dam to protect downstream bridges. The dam rises 155 feet above the North Fork of the American River and forms a 3.5-mile-long lake that has a surface of 280 acres. Old Foresthill Bridge is the first low bridge below the dam and that is where the trailhead for this hike is located. The trail extends along the path of the old Auburn–Foresthill Turnpike as it follows the contour of the slopes above the south side

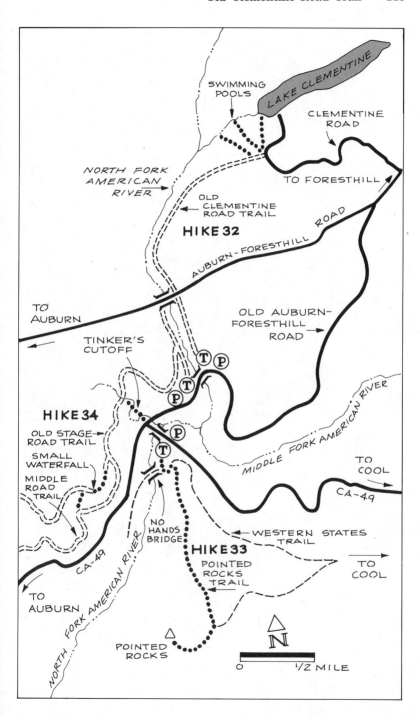

Fir and pine rise high above hillside trails.

of the North Fork of the American River. The rocks that were exposed along the turnpike are the remains of an ancient seabed, and you can see the defined layers that are typical of sedimentary rocks. Over geological time the seabed was uplifted and tilted to the west and deep gorges were cut in the uplifted slopes by raging waters. The American River, with its north, middle, and south forks, is only one of sixteen rivers that drain the west slope of the Sierra Nevada mountain range, but it became one of the most famous when gold was discovered along its banks in 1848. The roaring waters from the snowmelt above carried soil and gravel rich with minerals, including placer gold from quartz veins along the riverbanks, downstream where it was deposited over many thousands and millions of years. You can envision how the banks of the river along here must have looked during the peak of the gold rush.

Take the Old Auburn–Foresthill Road off CA-49 just less than 2 miles east of Auburn, and park in the parking area on the west side of the Old Foresthill Bridge. Walk across the bridge to the trailhead and take a left to head upstream.

The wide, flat trail follows along above the river for the first 0.5 mile as it passes beneath steep slopes that were denuded by fire in the summer of 1992. This fire was small by California standards, but was intense enough to completely destroy all vegetation on the hill-sides. This being chaparral country, with plants that respond to fire by quickly sprouting long-dormant seeds and regenerating from roots that were beneath the top layer of soil, growth has come back quickly to help inhibit erosion. Have the children see if they can see where the fire line for this fire extends up the slope.

The trail moves away from the river at just about 0.5 mile as it passes beneath the new Foresthill Bridge, which spans the canyon hundreds of feet overhead.

Between 0.5 and 1 mile, you and the children can look at the exposed rocks and explore the sedimentary layers that were laid down in long-gone seas that once covered this area. Have the children imagine what the area looked like during those eras when the hills above were much lower and stood beside a large sea.

By 0.75 mile the trail curves back near the river, where there is some access, but have the children wait for a while to go down to the water because there is much better access later on.

At 1 mile the trail curves uphill and away from the river as it heads for Clementine Road, where it ends at about 1.25 miles. From here there are several spur trails that lead down to beautiful pools and beaches along the river below the North Fork Dam. The most popular of these is the deep pool beneath the waterfall formed by the overflow of the North Fork Dam.

Swimming and wading are both popular here, but caution all swimmers about the undertow close to the waterfall.

After playing around the river (maybe panning for gold), and eating a snack or picnic lunch, return to the trailhead by the same route.

33. Pointed Rocks Trail

Type: Dayhike
Difficulty: Difficult for children
Distance: 5 miles, round trip
Hiking time: 6 hours
Elevation gain: 600 feet
Hikable: Year-round
Map: Auburn State Recreation Area

Any climb out of the deep American River Gorge is difficult, but you can avoid some of the strain by using switchbacks to make the climb less steep. The trail to Pointed Rocks does not do that. It follows along a route cleared by the telephone company as it buried a telephone cable. As a result, it simply follows the straightest line to the top of the ridge above the river. Why, then, would anyone want to take such a rigorous hike? Maybe because they want the physical test and want to see just how they match up against a hard climb. Or, just as likely, because it is the easiest way to reach the rock formations and ridge where the best views in the Auburn State Recreation Area are found. Among the oak and pine forests and open meadows along the ridge, deer can often be seen, and on a clear day you can see all the way to the Coast Range, including Mount Diablo in western Contra Costa County, or look up and down the Sacramento Valley for Folsom Reservoir and both the Sierra and Sutter buttes. I suggest that you not attempt this hike with children under ten years of age.

 Take CA-49 to just less than 2 miles east of Auburn, just past Old Auburn–Foresthill Road. Cross the bridge over the North Fork of the American River. Park along CA-49 on the east side of the river. Follow the Western States Trail toward No Hands Bridge downstream. (See map on page 115.)

Follow the river for about 200 yards to the No Hands Bridge. You come to a junction just before the bridge. Take a left and follow the trail as it heads uphill, and at about 0.25 mile the trail splits again. Take the right fork, the Pointed Rocks Trail, which begins its steep climb up the ridge.

From 0.25 mile to 0.75 mile, you make a continuous climb up the ridge as the trail passes through a pine and oak forest. The views are limited here, and the climb is taxing. Help get everyone over the hump by talking about what the view will be like when you come to the first small saddle in the ridge at 0.75 mile. There you can take a rest break as the children look out over the bridges below, and the

Butterflies and bees enjoy the nectar of wildflowers.

American River as it heads past Auburn to the site of a dam the Bureau of Reclamation has been attempting to build for the past several decades. Have the children guess how much of the river canyon will be flooded if the dam is ever built.

After the rest stop, the trail continues at a steady climb, but at a somewhat smaller gradient than that of the first 0.75 mile. There are also open meadows at sporadic intervals, where the view expands as you go higher and higher.

Have the children keep an eye out for deer as you climb, and have them see if they can spot a change in vegetation as you get higher. There should be fewer oaks and more pines, with ponderosa pine becoming more dominant.

By about 2 miles a spur of the Western States Trail comes in from the left, but continue to your right as the trail heads out to the pointed rocks formation at about 2.5 miles.

You can take a much-needed rest here as you look out over the Sacramento Valley. You can discuss the gold rush days, and the pioneers who helped settle California, as you eat and rest.

Remember to take plenty of water on this hike, even if you don't think that it is going to be extra warm.

You can return by the same route for a 5-mile round trip, or you can take the spur to the Western States Trail, which follows a less steep grade—though a longer trail—back to the No Hands Bridge for a 6-mile round trip.

34. Old Stage Road Trail

Type: Dayhike
Difficulty: Difficult for children
Distance: 3 miles, loop
Hiking time: 2 hours
Elevation gain: 500 feet
Hikable: Year-round
Map: Auburn State Recreation Area

The hillsides on both sides of the American River Canyon were crisscrossed with trails and roads during the years of the gold rush. As the large congregation of miners dispersed after the placer mines played out, many of these trails fell in disuse, but some remained to provide transit for the many small communities that survived long after the gold. Auburn and Foresthill were two of these communities, and the route between the two has changed slowly over the years as engineering and road-building techniques improved. Today there is a fairly level and straight road between them that crosses high over the North Fork of the American River on a modern bridge that rides far above any floodwaters. This hike in the Auburn State Recreation area takes you along the remains of several older routes that were used in the days before paved roads became a necessity to modern travelers.

Follow directions to the Old Foresthill Bridge given in hike 32, Old Clementine Road Trail (map on page 115). Park on the west side of the Old Foresthill Bridge.

Begin the hike by following the fire road upriver toward the new Foresthill Bridge. This trail leads to one of the most popular swimming holes along the river at Clark's Pool. Before you get to the new bridge, however, take a left onto the Old Stage Road Trail at 0.25 mile, and begin a steep climb up toward Auburn. Old Stage Road Trail enters at an oblique angle, and you must take a sharp left as you enter it.

Have the children look at the outcroppings of shale that jut out from the road cut. These are the remains of an old sea floor that was deposited in the region millions of years ago before the uplifting and tilting that created the Sierra Nevada occurred. Have them talk about how strong these movements must have been. (In the late 1800s there was an earthquake that was so strong that it lifted many parts of the Sierra by as much as 13 feet.)

Watch for poison oak along the road.

Soaring vultures and raptors, as well as the river canyon below, offer interesting views as you hike along the old road. At about 0.7 mile a creek crosses beneath the road via a culvert, and several large oak trees offer shade for a rest stop here. There is no outstanding view of the river from here, and brambles keep the children away from the creek, so this will be a short stop.

After the creek there is another outcropping of rock, but this one does not show the layering of sediments. The children may be interested in climbing, but there is abundant poison oak growing in and around the rocks that should deter them.

At 0.75 mile a small trail leads off downhill. This is the Tinker's Cut-Off Trail, and it leads down to the CA-49 Bridge. If you feel this hike is going to be too strenuous for any in your party, this is a good turnaround spot, as well as the last one. Take it for a 1-mile loop.

This hike continues on uphill, however, until a road enters from the right at 0.9 mile. The Old Stage Road Trail makes a sharp right turn here as it leads around the contour of the hill. The road that continues straight ahead becomes the Middle Road Trail. Take the right-hand trail.

As Old Stage Road Trail follows the contour of the hill, you have a good view of the new Foresthill Bridge, and you come to an area with some ponderosa pine. This species of pine grows at higher elevations, and this is about as low as it thrives.

By 1 mile you come to a thick growth of blackberries on both sides of the trail. Have the children watch out for the prickly vines, as well as the poison oak vines that grow intertwined with the blackberries.

You enter a good stand of manzanita by 1.25 miles. Have the children feel the smooth bark and tap on the hard wood. Discuss how chaparral plants are hard and prickly as a way of surviving the extreme heat of summer on these exposed hillsides.

Squirrels are frequently interested in the hikers who walk through their domain.

As you leave the manzanita you come to a drainage area where there are some exposed, flat rocks that are covered with dry moss in the summer and fall, but which are slick with green moss and running water after the winter rains come. The children will like to explore the rocks, but caution them about rattlesnakes in the summer and fall, although they should be easily seen, and about slippery conditions on the rocks in the winter and spring.

There is a small waterfall just below the trail when the weather is wet.

The trail splits at 1.3 miles. Take a left as you stay on Old Stage Road Trail. For the next several hundred yards you go through a dense thicket of chaparral.

At 1.4 miles there is a small bench downhill from the trail, where you can look out over the confluence of the North and Middle forks of the American River. You can stop here for a short rest.

The trail becomes a fire road after the bench, and at 1.6 miles a lightly used trail leads downhill through dense undergrowth to the Middle Road Trail, reached at 1.7 miles. Take a left onto this trail as you begin to head back downhill.

Just before 2 miles there are some outcroppings of serpentine, California's state rock, that you may have the children explore. This rock is formed by pressure where two tectonic plates join, and is found in very few places in the world outside California.

Several hundred yards downhill there are more rocks along the trail, and by 2.2 miles there is a large slab of rock laying against the hillside against another outcropping, and the children will like to explore beneath it. Check before they enter it, however, because this is an excellent place to find rattlesnakes.

The Middle Road Trail rejoins the Old Stage Road Trail at about 2.25 miles, and at just under 2.5 miles you come to the Tinker's Cut-Off Trail. You have the option of returning to the parking area by the route you came on Old Stage Road Trail.

However, the hike described here heads downhill on Tinker's Cut-Off Trail, the narrow path that leads through low-lying oaks and chaparral with several piles of rock outcroppings, where you should be on the lookout for rattlesnakes. The children will undoubtedly be frightened by a lizard or two scuttling about.

At about 2.5 miles the trail comes to a creek, where there is a good-size waterfall in wet winters and spring, and where there is a pool of clear, cool water even in the fall of dry years. This pool is clear, but don't let the children drink out of it. They can search for the crawdads and small fish that live here, though.

The trail leads through some large trees with ponderosa and digger pine as it continues downhill, and crosses the stream again at about 2.75 miles.

You come to CA-49 at 2.8 miles, where you take a left onto Old Foresthill Road and follow it toward the Old Foresthill Bridge, where you return to your vehicle at 3 miles.

35. Spenceville Wildlife Area Dry Creek Trail Loop

Type: Dayhike
Difficulty: Moderate for children
Distance: 2.25 miles, loop
Hiking time: 2 hours
Elevation gain: Minimal
Hikable: Year-round
Map: California Department of Fish and Game

This 11,213-acre wildlife area is one of several operated by the California Department of Fish and Game throughout the state, where various wildlife is protected and managed. This management area was once part of the large Beale Air Force Base, which bounds it on the west, and runs from just south of Smartville on CA-20 to the north to just above Camp Far West Reservoir to the south. Most of the area is open grassland with blue, valley, and live oaks, and there is little water. There are several seasonal streams, however, along with about forty springs and three small reservoirs, scattered throughout the area, and one year-round stream—Dry Creek—that bisects the management area from east to west along Spenceville Road. The marked trails in the management area are primarily used by equestrians, but hikers are welcome, and traffic is so limited that even hiking along the improved roads is excellent.

You can enter the management area from the north by taking CA-20 to Smartville Road and then turning left onto the improved gravel Waldo Road at the area boundary, or from the south from I-80 by taking CA-65 to Sheridan and then taking Long Ravine Road north past Camp Far West Reservoir. Either way involves driving on about 5 miles of improved gravel road to the trailhead at the junction of Spenceville and Long Ravine roads. Park at the information bulletin board where Long Ravine Road dead ends into Spenceville Road.

From the bulletin board, head west on Spenceville Road. The road drops gently down toward Dry Creek, which can be seen to the north,

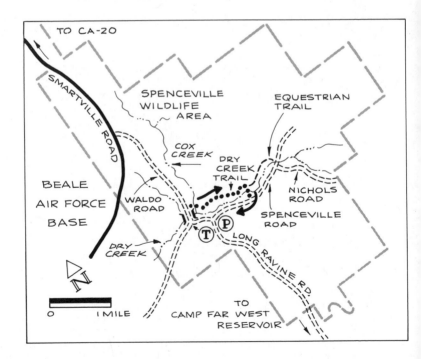

Streams provide much-needed water to sustain riparian growth through hot, dry summers.

and just before 0.5 mile, Waldo Road enters from the right. Take a right on Waldo Road and cross an old metal bridge at 0.5 mile.

The children can watch the water as it flows beneath the bridge and try to see if they can spot any fish in the clear water. They can gauge how fast the creek is flowing by dropping a leaf or light stick into the water.

Continue across the bridge for another 100 yards to the equestrian trail that crosses Waldo Road. There is a gate in the fence, but it is likely to be locked. Climb through the fence on the right side of the road to begin the trail. At this point, the trail is a fire road that passes through a level section of open grassland, and is separated from the creek by a barbed wire fence.

At about 0.75 mile the trail crosses a marshy area that is part of a seasonal tributary of Dry Creek. During wet weather you may have to hunt for an easy place to cross, and may have to head upstream around the marsh, but most of the year you should be able to cross with no difficulty.

Have the children listen and look for birds that live in marshes, such as the redwing blackbird, as you cross the area. You may even want to hike upstream a short way to look for other marsh animals such as frogs and dragonflies.

You continue through open grassland with an occasional oak, and by 1 mile you reach a heavier stand of oak and get closer to the creek, which has a thick riparian growth along its banks. You can let the children explore along the edge of the creek anywhere along here.

Large boulders of serpentine, California's state rock, are exposed along the trail between 1 and 1.25 miles, and the children may want to explore around them. Warn them about rattlesnakes, however, and make sure they look before they reach or step near the rocks. There are more outcroppings of serpentine in the floodplain of the creek to the right of the trail.

There are plenty of willow along the creek, and the children can see how many different kinds they can identify.

At 1.25 miles there is a large open pool in the creek, where the children can wade or explore. There are always plenty of birds in the trees and brush along the creek.

At 1.3 miles the trail dead ends into another trail at a T junction. Take a right as you head toward the creek. After about 100 yards you cross the creek. You either have to do some rock-hopping or wade across the creek. There is a good flow even during late summer. The children may want to take a break here to have a snack and explore along the banks of the creek among the alders and sedges.

From the creek the trail heads toward Spenceville Road, and crosses it just before 1.5 miles. There is an old fig tree along the south side of the road about 100 feet after the trail crossing that has excellent figs in late summer. Have the children watch for poison oak if they attempt to pick the figs, however.

Follow Spenceville Road back to the parking area to complete a 2.25-mile loop.

For a 3-mile loop, take a left at the T junction before crossing the creek at 1.3 miles, and continue on the equestrian trail until it curves across the creek at 1.5 mile or so and meets Spenceville Road at Nichols Road.

36. Sutter National Wildlife Refuge Levee Trail

Type: Dayhike
Difficulty: Moderate for children
Distance: 3 miles, round trip
Hiking time: 2 hours
Elevation gain: Minimal
Hikable: Year-round
Map: USGS Gilsizer and Tisdale Weir Quads

The Sacramento Valley is a vital stop-off for migrating waterfowl as they follow the Pacific Flyway each fall. While flights of birds once numbered in the tens of millions, they now are limited to tens or hundreds of thousands. This dramatic reduction in numbers has occurred for several reasons, one of which has been the almost total destruction of wetlands in the valley. North of Sacramento there are several state and national wildlife refuges that have been set aside to help preserve feeding sites for the still large flocks of migrating waterfowl, and one of these is the Sutter National Wildlife Refuge, which is located in the mile-wide Sutter Bypass to the southwest of

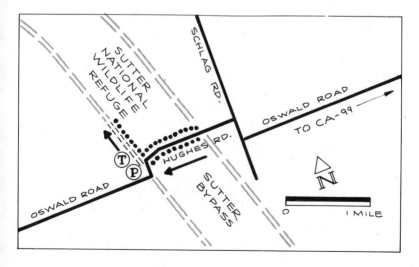

The Sutter Buttes, claimed to be the smallest mountain range in the world, rise from the Sacramento Valley.

Marysville. Before Oroville and Shasta dams were constructed on the Sacramento and Feather rivers, floods regularly inundated large areas of land on both sides of the rivers. To help prevent rich farmlands and heavily populated areas from being flooded, several large bypasses (Sutter and Yolo) were built in the upper Sacramento Valley. Restraining levees were built in areas that most frequently flooded each winter on each side of the bypasses to help channel floodwaters downstream on the rising rivers away from populated areas. These are no longer as important in restraining the waters of the rivers, but 2,931 acres of the Sutter Bypass designated as a national wildlife refuge are now flooded each winter to provide resting and feeding areas for migrating waterfowl.

From CA-99 near Marysville, take Oswald Road west until it dead ends into Schlag Road. Turn right on Schlag Road and continue for several hundred yards, and then turn left on Hughes Road. Continue on Hughes Road as it crosses the east levee of the Sutter Bypass and drops down into the bypass itself. Cross the bypass and park on the road atop the west levee. Do not block access to the levee road. Because the bypass may be closed during the winter, call the wildlife refuge (916-934-2801) to determine if the road is open.

From the parking area head north along the levee. The mountains directly ahead of you are the Sutter Buttes, and are known as the smallest mountain range in the world. Have the children guess how the range was developed. They were once part of a much larger range that rose from the much lower floor of what is now the Sacramento Valley, and as the valley filled with sediment, only the very top of these mountains remained.

The best time to take this hike is during the fall migration of waterfowl, which peaks in late November and December, when you can see large flocks of ducks and geese. The large flights of Canada geese are particularly impressive as they come in for a landing or take-off. With thousands of birds in the air at one time, you can feel as well as hear the power of nature.

If you are hiking during this time, have the children keep a watch out for waterfowl in the fields to the west as well as the refuge to the east.

Continue along the top of the levee for about 0.5 mile as you watch for birds, and then return. If it is not too wet, climb down the slope of the levee and walk back on the fire road near the slough that separates the refuge from the levee.

The growth along the slough is full of wildlife throughout the year, and provides nesting sites for numerous small birds during the spring. Have the children keep an eye and ear out for these birds as they walk along, as well as for nesting boxes that have been placed in some of the trees for wood ducks. These boxes have been built to replace the natural nesting places that have been lost as old snags and dead trees have slowly disappeared from riparian growth due to human intervention.

In the occasional break in the riparian growth, you may also see large water birds such as herons and egrets during most of the year.

You return to the parking area at 1 mile. If you wish to stop hiking you can do so now, but this hike takes a closer look at the large flocks of waterfowl during the fall. Take a left and hike along the side of Hughes Road as it crosses the refuge. Although you cannot walk out into the refuge itself, you can hike along the road.

A pair of binoculars will give you closeup views of the large geese as you cross the refuge. Have the children see how many different types of geese and ducks they can identify. (They don't have to know their names, and can group them according to their own means.)

You reach the east levee at 2 miles. Return back along the road to the parking area for a 3-mile round trip.

Hikes Within 40 to 60 Miles of Downtown Sacramento

Overnight hikes are a great introduction to nature for adults and children alike.

37. Smittle Creek Trail

Type: Dayhike
Difficulty: Easy for children
Distance: 1.5 miles, loop
Hiking time: 1 hour
Elevation gain: Minimal
Hikable: Year-round
Map: US Bureau of Reclamation

Monticello Dam was built on Putah Creek between Napa and Winters in the 1950s as a flood control and irrigation project by the US Bureau of Reclamation. Lake Berryessa formed behind the dam, and inundated the small community of Monticello. During the drought years in the late 1980s and early 1990s, the lake fell low enough so boaters could actually see the ghostly remains of the community's buildings beneath the water. Although this large lake has been a mecca for fishermen, boaters, and water-skiers, little trail building has been done around its shoreline. In stark contrast to the almost 100 miles of trails that have been built around Folsom Lake, a comparably sized bureau project, there are only 2.6 miles of developed trails around Lake Berryessa. This is unfortunate, because the area is ideal for outings during the sunny days of winter when forested regions are too damp and dank for pleasant hiking. Nevertheless, the one developed trail on the lake offers a pleasant hike along the shore through open grassland and oak woodland where birds, wildflowers, and mammals such as deer may be seen in abundance.

Take CA-121 north from Napa to CA-128 (which comes from Winters to the east) and turn northwest toward Knoxville Road. Turn north on Knoxville Road (also known as Spanish Flat Road) and continue for about 5 miles to the Smittle Creek Picnic Area. The trail leads out of the south end of the parking area.

Smittle Creek sits almost directly across the lake from the old Monticello townsite. A good growth of oak woodland covers the hills above the lake, and the trail follows the contour of the shoreline as it curves in and out around the hills that jut out into the lake.

From the parking lot, you cross a wooden footbridge after about 100 yards, and then follow the trail as it heads uphill from the shoreline.

The trail reaches the end of the first small peninsula at about 0.3 mile, and then turns in around another inlet as it drops down to cross another wooden footbridge just before 0.4 mile. As you cross the bridge at the tip of the inlet, the trail climbs back up to the next ridge.

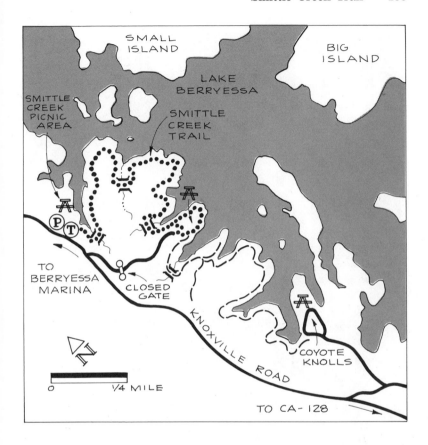

This hike can be very hot during the summer months, and you should beware of rattlesnakes most of the year. More likely you and the children will be more frightened by lizards scurrying through the dry grass, however, than by real rattlesnakes.

Among the oaks you can see a number of digger pines that rise above the oaks, and scattered along the trail are good specimens of manzanita. Have the children feel the smooth bark and hard wood of this chaparral plant. Have them look at the small, hard leaves, and discuss how these help the plant survive in hot, dry summers by keeping evaporation down.

Manzanita means "little apple" in Spanish, and got its name from the small, applelike fruit that appears on the plants in late summer. Both Native Americans and European pioneers used this nutritious fruit during times when other food was scarce. The children may taste them if any are on the plants.

At about 0.75 mile the trail again circles around a creek-fed inlet

Bridges cross dry seasonal streams that become roaring torrents of water during heavy winter storms.

where a small wooden footbridge crosses the creek. This is a good place for the children to explore a creek if there is any water running. The bridge is low, and the creek is accessible, although there is some poison oak on the banks.

Uphill from the creek are several California buckeyes, which have

beautiful clumps of white flowers in the spring that turn into the
largest seed of any tree in North America. This tree is a migrant from
more tropical climates, and has adapted to the hot, dry summers of
Northern California by going into dormancy at the first sign of heat,
and staying dormant until the next winter. Children like to play with
the hard seed pods that can get as big as tennis balls. They drop from
the trees from early to late fall after their green cover has shed.

At 1 mile the trail forks, with the left fork heading out to the
tip of a peninsula. Take this fork and follow as it leads to a bench
near the tip, where you can rest and look out over the lake. If it is
a time of high water in the lake, the children can play along the shore
as you rest.

The trail continues around the tip of the peninsula, and returns
to join with the right fork at a picnic area with rest rooms and water.

From the picnic area, the trail leads along a paved road back to
Knoxville Road, where you take a right to return to the Smittle Picnic
Area at 1.5 miles.

For a longer hike, you can continue up the trail to Coyote Knolls,
which is a 5-mile round trip.

38. Lakes Trail Loop

Type: Dayhike
Difficulty: Moderate for children
Distance: 2.5 miles, loop
Hiking time: 2 hours
Elevation gain: 300 feet
Hikable: Year-round
Map: Fairfield Department of Parks
and Recreation

Rockville Hills Regional Park is a little-known gem of a park that
lies in the hills to the west of Fairfield, overlooking the city and the
farmlands and marshlands to the east. The 450-mile-long Bay Ridge
Trail, which is in the planning stage (with about one-third of the trails
actually in place in late 1992), will run through Rockville Hills Regional
Park when it is completed. The park has two lakes (one is more of
a small pond) and plenty of oak woodland. During the spring, wildflowers are bountiful on the hillsides, and birds are lively and chatty
as they prepare for mating season. Watch overhead for courting raptors

such as redtail hawks and an occasional golden eagle as they perform their mating rituals.

Take the Rockville Road exit off I-80 in Fairfield and head west for 3 miles to Suisun Valley Road. Continue on Rockville Road for about 1 mile past Suisun Valley Road to the park entrance on the left. The trail begins at the rear of the parking lot.

The trail begins an immediate steep climb as you head around the contour of a hill. For the first 0.25 mile, you hike through oak woodland and then come into an open area where there are excellent views out over the flat lands to the east.

At about 0.5 mile, after you have made a steep 300-foot climb, the trail levels out and crosses a paved park-maintenance road. Continue straight ahead across the paved road and after about 200 yards you come to a small pond on the left. There is a picnic table beneath a large oak tree beside the pond, and children like to explore around the shallow edges in search of frogs and tadpoles, as well as dragonflies and small birds.

After a short rest, return to the main trail and head right, toward a larger lake, which you reach at 0.75 mile after a short climb.

For a slightly longer hike that gives views to the southwest of the park, you can take the trail that leads off to the left, which winds around a knoll and rejoins the main trail at the upper lake.

Shortly after you reach the lake, the trail forks; stay left and continue to the upper end of the lake. There are picnic tables above the lake, and this is an excellent place to stop for a long lunch break while the children explore around the edges of the lake, where the shallow water is home to many small birds and water animals. Although the children should not attempt to swim in the lake, they

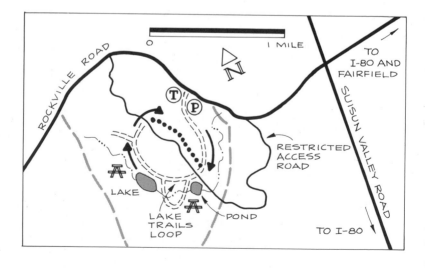

Lakes and ponds are excellent rest stops along hot trails.

can wade in the shallows as they search among the reeds and rushes.

After a stop at the lake you have the option of returning by the same route for a 1.5-mile round trip. The hike described here, however, takes you along the east side of the lake, on the main trail, which continues north.

At about 1 mile the trail moves away from the lake (the upper end of the lake is marshy, and the children may want to explore a little there before they leave the area).

The trail follows below a ridge north of the lake, and there are a number of rock outcroppings that you can explore around. Remember to follow proper rattlesnake precautions by always knowing where you are stepping, and never placing your hands in places you cannot see first.

The trail leads through open grassland dotted with several types of oaks. You can have the children attempt to group the oaks by their leaf color, type of leaves, and type of acorns.

At about 1.25 miles the trail forks, with the left fork bending around the ridge you have been following and the right fork heading uphill back toward the parking lot. Take the right fork and continue uphill.

At about 1.5 miles the trail crosses the paved road, and then another trail. Take a right on the trail, and follow it along the ridge back toward the first small pond. If the trail is wet and muddy, you can take the paved road, for they join near the pond.

The children can explore around the many rock outcroppings that are alongside the trail on the ridge, and see if the rocks are all the same types or if there are several different types represented.

At about 2 miles you rejoin the main trail that you came uphill on. The small pond is to your right across the meadow.

Take a left and head back downhill to the parking lot at 2.5 miles.

39. Suisun Marsh Trail

Type: Dayhike
Difficulty: Moderate for children
Distance: 2 miles, loop
Hiking time: 2 hours
Elevation gain: None
Hikable: Year-round
Map: Solano County Farmlands and Open Space Foundation

The Solano County Farmlands and Open Space Foundation works with the agricultural community of the region to preserve agricultural land as a productive resource protected from the pressures of development. It also purchases land to help protect and restore marshlands and riparian habitats throughout the county. Rush Ranch is an old ranch that has been purchased by the foundation, and opened to the public as an educational and recreational resource. The 2,070-acre open space preserve sits along the 84,000-acre Suisun Marsh, the largest single estuarine marsh in the United States with 55,000 acres of wetlands and 29,000 acres of bays and sloughs. In addition to having three developed trails and an education center, Rush Ranch is still a working cattle ranch, with a controlled program oriented around wildlife habitat management.

From I-80 in Fairfield, head southeast on CA-12. Just to the east of Suisun City, take Grizzly Island Road south from CA-12 for 2 miles.

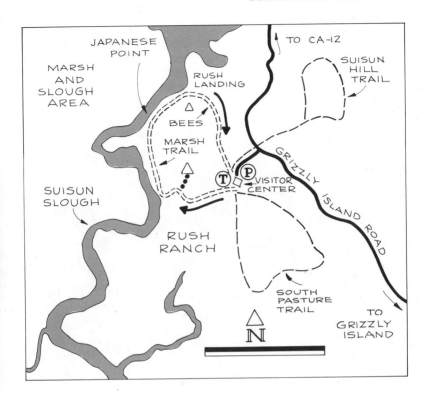

Park near the Rush Ranch visitor center. The Marsh Trail begins behind the visitor center.

This is a marked nature trail, and brochures are generally available at the visitor center. You may want to call (707-421-1351) before your trip to obtain the self-guiding brochure, however, because they are often out at the center.

The trail heads toward a row of planted eucalyptus, and through a pasture area, toward a small hill and the marsh.

At 0.25 mile the trail forks and heads around a small knoll. Follow the signs to the left. After about 100 feet a spur trail leads to the top of the knoll, from where you can get a good overview of the marsh. Take this short side trip so the children can see where they are headed, and maybe see some of the many birds that live in the marsh.

Return to the main trail from the knoll and take a right to continue around to the marsh.

The trail immediately enters the marsh area as it curves around the knoll, and the children can begin to look for waterfowl and other water-loving birds as you enter an area of ponds and sloughs. Although you can see many different types of birds here year-round, late fall is a prime time to see thousands and thousands of migrating

Many trails pass by water-bird nesting and feeding sites.

birds that sometimes cover all open water in the ponds and small sloughs.

Have the children see how many different types of birds they can see on the walk through the marsh area. In the fall this might reach to more than 50, because there have been more than 230 different species of birds identified in the area.

They may also see small mammals such as muskrats and river otters along the pond edges if they keep a sharp eye out for them.

At 0.5 mile the trail takes a sharp right turn and heads up the banks of Suisun Slough, a broad, open body of water that is more like a river than a slough. Continue along the slough, all the while watching for different birds.

Just before you reach 1 mile, the trail curves near Japanese Point, and heads toward a small knoll at 1.25 miles. There you can climb to the top for another vista of the surrounding marsh and pastureland. Rush Landing, where boats and barges serving the surrounding ranches landed until well into the twentieth century, is located just around the knoll.

After you round the knoll you head into open pastureland and away from the marsh. Continue to your right, and at about 1.5 miles you cross a dirt dam across a small drainage area. Just beyond the dam there is a digger bee colony. These bees are not aggressive, so you can safely observe them as they enter and leave their nesting areas.

From 1.5 to 2 miles the trail continues across open pasture, and the children can get a closeup look at the living area of some of the residents of such regions. By getting down on their hands and knees and crawling along the trail, they can look for small tunnels in the matted grass on the side of the trail. These tunnels are made by voles and mice as they scurry out onto the open trail to eat fallen seeds. They don't stay out in the open for any extended time, because the hawks that soar overhead are always on the lookout for an easy meal.

The trail returns to the parking lot at 2 miles.

There are two other trails at Rush Ranch that give you a very different perspective of the region. The Suisun Hill Trail takes you into some high hills to the east of the marshlands, where you get an excellent overview of the ranch, and the South Pasture Trail takes you into an area that was partially reclaimed from the marsh.

40. Duck Pond Levee Trail

Type: Dayhike
Difficulty: Moderate for children
Distance: 1.5 miles, loop
Hiking time: 1 hour
Elevation gain: None
Hikable: Year-round
Map: California Department of Fish and Game

Grizzly Island sits at the edge of Suisun Bay, where it is often difficult to tell what is land and what is water, and where it is impossible to get away from the constant winds that blow off the bay after they pass through the Carquinez Straits. In the latter part of the nineteenth century, farmers tried to reclaim the marshlands by surrounding large areas with levees, but nature wasn't always cooperative, and the sloughs often filled with salt or brackish water just when the farmers needed freshwater for irrigation. By the 1930s the farmers were more than agreeable when the state began to buy up huge chunks of the marshlands as a winter wildlife protection area, and private interests bought other parcels for development as duck hunting clubs. Today the state owns almost 15,000 acres in the area, and these are home to an astounding variety of wildlife. You may see five or six species of ducks, several of geese, a number of wading birds, owls, harriers, redtail hawks, great blue herons, pheasants, river otters, muskrats, snakes, and tule elk as you hike along the levees. If you are lucky you may even see the reclusive and endangered salt marsh harvest mouse. Grizzly Island Game Refuge is open for hiking and nature study from about February 1 to September 15 each year, and for hunting during the rest of the time. Some areas are off limits to hikers during hunting season, and you can call (707-425-3828) for conditions and hiking limitations, as well as maps and brochures.

Follow directions to the previous hike (see hike 39, Suisun Marsh Trail) to Grizzly Island Road. Continue on Grizzly Island Road for 14 miles from Suisun City to the game refuge's headquarters. Register there before heading into the refuge itself.

After registering, continue along Grizzly Island Road and King

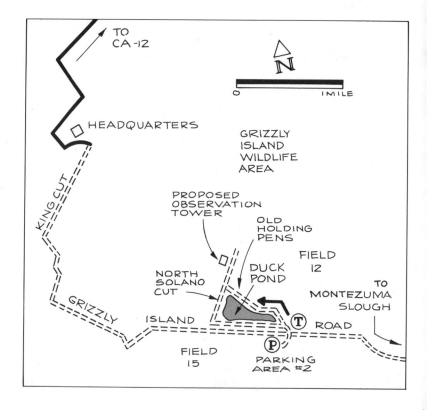

Nesting boxes for wood ducks have been installed in many places to replace the wooden snags that are the favorite nesting sites for these ducks.

Cut Road to parking area 2 for this hike. (If this area is closed, you may continue on Grizzly Island Road to its end, where there is parking along the levee of Montezuma Slough. You can hike along the levee year-round.)

Park and walk across the road to the levee that surrounds the duck pond. Take the levee that goes to the right around the pond. There is a slough between this road and the open field to the east. There are waterfowl in the pond year-round, but the busiest times are spring nesting, the raising of the young in early summer, and fall migration. Hiking is limited during parts of the fall migration, but not during other times.

As you walk along the levee, the children can see how many different birds they can spot both in the pond and along the banks of the slough to the east. They can also keep an eye out for the largest mammal found in the management area. This is the tule elk, which, though the smallest elk native to North America, reaches a whopping 800 pounds when full-grown.

These elk were native to the island, but disappeared in the late 1800s, and were absent until the state reintroduced them to the region in 1977. Today the herd is strong and thriving at about 100 elk.

If you are hiking along this trail in the late summer or early fall you may hear the elk bugling as they anticipate the mating season. They have velvet antlers during this time, and they can often be seen rubbing them on trees or power poles.

Just before 0.75 mile the levee comes to a grove of eucalyptus trees on the east side of the slough, and this is where the elk were acclimated to the island when they were first reintroduced in 1977. The pens are still visible as you look across the slough, as are nesting boxes for wood ducks.

At 0.75 mile the levee ends at the North Solano Cut. There are plans for an observation tower where visitors can watch for roaming elk just to the northeast of the eucalyptus grove, but until that is completed, take a left on North Solano Cut and hike along the northwest end of the duck pond back toward Grizzly Island Road.

At 1 mile you reach the road. Here you have a choice of walking along the levee between the pond and the road, or walking along the road itself, until you reach the parking area at 1.5 miles.

41. Benicia State Recreation Area Marsh Trail Loop

Type: Dayhike
Difficulty: Easy for children
Distance: 1.25 miles, loop
Hiking time: 1 hour
Elevation gain: Minimal
Hikable: Year-round
Map: Benicia State Recreation Area

The main feature of Benicia State Park is the historic district with the old state capital. A less known part of the park, but still popular with local residents, is the more than 2,000-acre wetlands designated as the Benicia State Recreation Area. This area lies just to the west of downtown Benicia, and includes a large inlet off the north side of the Carquinez Strait, directly opposite the Carquinez Strait Regional Shoreline. These wetlands are home to many water-

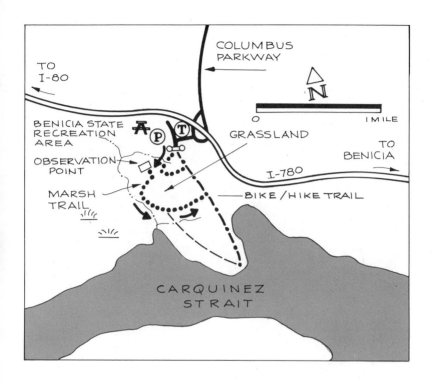

fowl and wading birds, as well as a popular stopover and feeding site for migrating waterfowl in the fall. Hikers can walk out into the edge of the marshlands to observe the wildlife.

From I-80 south of Fairfield, take I-780 southeast. In Benicia, take the Columbus Parkway exit off I-780 and follow signs to the recreation area. Park along the road outside the park entrance. Head southeast along the road past the closed vehicle gate and along the paved biking and jogging trail.

At about 0.1 mile a lightly used trail leads to the right off the paved trail. Take this to head down a slight slope, under the low limbs of a large willow, and through a patch of tules and cattails. Plenty of small birds live in this area year-round, but spring nesting season is when they are most obvious. Have the children see how many different birds they can spot. They don't have to know the names of the various birds, but can make up their own classification system (by color, size, where seen, et cetera).

During wet weather this trail is impassable, and you must continue along the paved biking and jogging trail to 0.3 mile where a well-marked trail leads to the right down toward the marsh through open grassland.

Contra Costa County parks offer plenty of open grasslands for winter hikes.

If you have taken the first side trail, it joins with the larger trail at just past 0.3 mile. Take a right at this junction and head toward the marsh.

After about another 50 yards there is a small spur trail to the right that leads to an overlook where the children can observe the creek that drains this section of the marsh. Please obey the signs and stay within the marked boundaries. This area is very fragile, and hikers are asked not to explore along the edge of the marsh or creek, to avoid further destruction of the habitat.

After spending time at the overlook, return to the main trail and take a right. At about 0.5 mile there are several medium-size boulders on both sides of the trail. Have the children explore around both those near the marsh and those on the drier, grassland side to see if they can find any small animals. If they do, have them see if there are any differences in the animals.

Although there is little danger of encountering rattlesnakes here, it is always a good idea to follow safe wilderness practices and watch for them.

Continue along the trail to about 0.7 mile, after the trail has curved to the left to circle an arm of the marsh. At that point a side trail leads to the right across a marshy area with rocks and driftwood that offer a route across the water. If you take this side trek, the trail leads up to grassland on the other side to the marshy area. You can follow this for some distance before it turns to the left and joins with the paved biking and jogging trail. This makes for about a 3-mile loop.

The children can explore around the rocks and driftwood even if you do not cross over the marsh. Have them see how many different small animals they can find and discuss how they may differ from the animals found in the grassland less than 100 feet away.

Return to the main trail and continue to the paved biking and jogging trail at 0.8 mile. Take a left and return to the parking area at 1.25 miles. There are some picnic tables past the entrance kiosk in the park.

42. Carquinez Overlook Loop Trail

Type: Dayhike
Difficulty: Easy for children
Distance: 2.5 miles, loop
Hiking time: 1 hour
Elevation gain: Minimal
Hikable: Year-round
Map: East Bay Regional Park

The Carquinez Strait Regional Shoreline includes bluffs and shorelines between Crockett and Martinez. The hills rise high above the water of Carquinez Strait, which is the gateway to the Sacramento/San Joaquin Delta. The regional shoreline is divided into two separate sections: Bull Valley Staging Area near Crockett, and Carquinez East Staging Area near Martinez; both are reached by Carquinez Scenic Drive. There is no through traffic between them, however, because a landslide in 1982 destroyed part of the road, and it has not been rebuilt. The trails in both sections of the regional shoreline provide excellent hikes for the fall and winter because they are exposed to the full sun most of the time.

Take I-80 and I-680 to Crockett. From Crockett, take Carquinez Scenic Drive east to the Bull Valley Staging Area. From the parking lot, go through the hikers' gate to the trailhead.

The Bull Valley Trail heads downhill to the left; instead, take the Carquinez Overlook Loop Trail to the right from the trailhead as it begins to follow the contour of the hills above Carquinez Strait.

The trail takes you through open grassland and overlooks Carquinez Strait, the hills on the opposite shore, and Benicia State

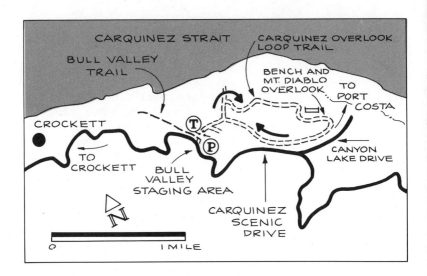

Recreation Area. The children will like to count the ships and boats that pass by below as you continue along the trail. You may have them keep track of what kinds of vessels they see. These will be everything from small pleasure boats to larger fishing boats to huge oil tankers that are heading to the refineries at Martinez and Antioch.

At 0.1 mile a lightly used trail leads off to the right. Take the main trail to the left.

As the trail leads around the hill, you can look back toward the Carquinez Bridge and see a number of deteriorating, abandoned docks with old fish-processing buildings. Discuss with the children why these were abandoned and talk about how large corporations have taken over the processing of fish that was once done by the individual fishermen.

At 0.25 mile the trail crosses a ravine and you can see a large stand of eucalyptus downhill. Coastal scrub chaparral replaces open grassland uphill from the trail along this section.

Just past 0.25 mile a trail leads off to the right. This is the return trail for the loop, so stay to the left as you continue around the hill.

There is plenty of birdlife along the trail most of the year, so have the children keep an eye out for large birds such as hawks and vultures that are often seen soaring above. Among the more interesting small birds that can be seen along the trail is the loggerhead shrike. This small black and gray bird has a beak that is hooked like a hawk's beak, and we called it the "butcher bird" in my youth. This came from its habit of storing its prey of voles and small mice on thorn trees or barbed wire fences.

Just past 0.5 mile, Mount Diablo and the George Miller Bridge that crosses the upper portion of Carquinez Strait near Antioch come into view.

A bench overlooks Port Costa and Mount Diablo just past 1 mile, and you can take a short break here as everyone enjoys the view.

The trail turns to the right and heads behind the top of the ridge. Along this section of the trail you overlook Port Costa and several grass-covered ridges that are dotted with thick stands of oak trees. During the winter the trail can be muddy along this section, so you may wish to return to the parking area the way you came rather than completing the loop.

At 2 miles the loop returns to the main trail above the eucalyptus grove. Continue back to the parking lot at about 2.5 miles.

An abandoned fishing wharf contrasts with a modern bridge in this view from the hills above Carquinez Strait.

43. Arch Bridge Trail Loop

Type: Dayhike
Difficulty: Easy for children
Distance: 1.25 miles, loop
Hiking time: 1 hour
Elevation gain: None
Hikable: Year-round
Map: Martinez Regional Shoreline

In 1974 the 343 acres in Martinez Regional Shoreline was a seldom-used marshlands and industrial fill area. In that year the Martinez Waterfront Planning Agency and the East Bay Regional Park District signed a joint powers agreement to develop three types of park facilities. These were recreational areas with fields and large open lawns, picnic and playground areas, and natural marshlands. Today there are more than 3 miles of hiking trails around and through the

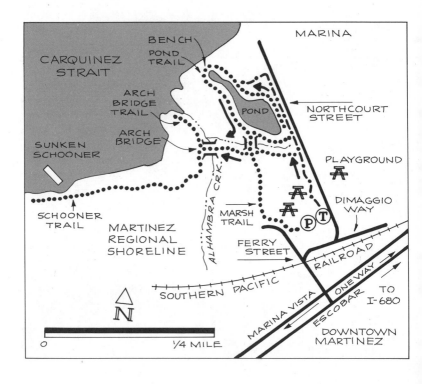

marshlands that offer peaceful, easy walks for everyone. Birdwatchers come to the marsh during the fall migration to look for water and shorebirds that are attracted to the open marshlands.

Take I-80 and I-680 to Martinez. In downtown Martinez, take Ferry Street across the Southern Pacific Railroad and turn right on DiMaggio Way. After a short block turn left on Northcourt Street, and then left again into the first parking area on the left.

From the parking lot follow the paved trail across a lawn area as it parallels Northcourt Street. Continue straight ahead on the paved trail past the trail that leads off toward the marsh at 0.1 mile. At about 0.2 mile a gravel trail leads off to the left of the paved trail to follow the south shoreline of the pond. Continue on the paved trail, which skirts the east side of the pond. Have the children see how many different kinds of water birds can be spotted around the pond.

As the trail leads around the pond, hikers have formed another trail closer to the water. This trail is not maintained, but it is a good spot to look for bird tracks in the mud. See how many different kinds of tracks the children can identify, and try to guess which birds made each kind.

At about 0.4 mile the trail circles around the north end of the pond, and there is a bench there for overlooking the waters of Carquinez Strait. During fall migration times you can see hundreds of water and shorebirds from here.

As you circle around the west side of the pond, there is a marsh on your right. From here you can see Arch Bridge and the remains of an old schooner in the distance.

At about 0.5 mile a boardwalk leads to the right across the marsh. Take this right turn and have the children closely observe the ooze and mud below; it contains millions of small plants and animals in each handful, and is a rich food supply for many birds and small marine animals. Be careful as you cross the boardwalk during the winter, because the boards become slippery during the rainy season.

After about 100 yards the boardwalk crosses a small creek by a bridge and joins another trail. Take a right to head toward Arch Bridge, which crosses Alhambra Creek at about 0.6 mile. At the foot of the bridge there are several informational plaques that tell about the cultural and natural history of the marshlands.

Cross over the bridge, which offers an excellent panorama of the marsh and the wrecked schooner to the left, and turn right. After about 50 yards you will see a number of pilings that are all that remain of an old fishing wharf. Talk to the children about how in earlier times there were many more small business operations in the fishing industry, and how many of these disappeared as mechanization came to the industry.

The trail continues toward the water, and ends at about 0.8 mile. Here you can explore the plants that live in the intertidal zone that

Arch Bridge rises above saltwater marshland.

is alternately covered with salt water and exposed to the air. This is also an excellent place to have the children look for footprints of various birds and small mammals.

Return to the bridge on the same trail. (If you want to take a longer walk, you can continue straight ahead on the trail instead of crossing the bridge, and continue across the marsh to the schooner. This can add from 1 to 1.5 miles to the hike. Along this section of the trail you are likely to spot low-flying marsh hawks, also known as harriers for their favorite prey. These hawks are easily identified by the white patch that can be seen on their rump just at the top end of their tail feathers.)

If you are ready to head back, cross over Alhambra Creek on the bridge. Continue straight ahead to the trail junction at about 1 mile. Take a right (a left takes you back across the boardwalk, and straight ahead takes you back to the paved trail) as the trail wanders along the edge of the marsh. Have the children keep an eye out for the many small birds that live and nest in the tules and taller marsh plants.

At about 1.2 miles you return to the lawn and picnic area near the parking lot, which is at 1.25 miles. If the children wish to play in a large playground while you have lunch, cross over Northcourt Street to the playground and picnic area.

---

44. Diablo View/Spengler/Alhambra Creek Trails Loop

Type: Dayhike
Difficulty: Difficult for children
Distance: 3 miles, loop
Hiking time: 2 hours
Elevation gain: 500 feet
Hikable: Year-round
Map: East Bay Regional Park

The 5,706-acre Briones Regional Park was acquired by the East Bay Regional Park District in 1964. The park was named for the Briones family, one of the early Spanish settlers in the region, who once owned the 13,316-acre Rancho Felipe. The grasslands of the Bear Creek watershed were used primarily for cattle grazing from the time of the first settlers, and in the early 1900s, much of the watershed land was purchased by the People's Water Company, which was later purchased by the East Bay Municipal Utility District (EBMUD). In 1957 Contra Costa County and EBMUD created a large open-space park in the Bear Creek watershed that was named Briones Park. The East Bay Regional Park District annexed the park in 1964, and has since expanded it to its present size. The park is largely undeveloped, and it is used primarily by hikers who walk the miles of scenic trails.

From I-80, take CA-4 southeast. From CA-4, take Alhambra Valley Road south and turn east on Reliez Valley Road. Follow the signs to the Alhambra Creek Valley Staging Area to the southwest of Reliez Valley Road.

From the parking lot go through the hikers' gate to the trailhead. Turn left onto the Diablo View Trail as it begins to head uphill through open grassland around the contour of a hill. After about 200 yards the Tavan Trail leads off to the left and the Diablo View Trail continues to the right. Stay on the Diablo View Trail.

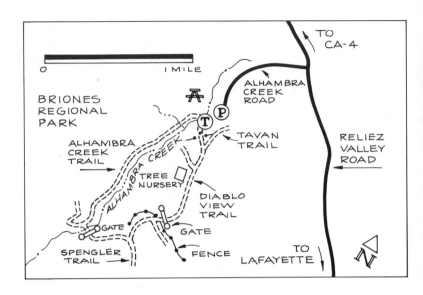

A ravine is on the left side of the trail as you head uphill, and during the winter it is often full of roaring water. During summer and fall it is empty, and children like to explore around the large rocks in the ravine.

During the spring these hillsides are brilliant fields of wildflowers that stand out against the green grass.

At about 0.3 mile there is a fenced-in area where the park grows young oaks. A fire road goes downhill to the right just before the fenced area, and one goes uphill straight ahead as it passes the tree nursery. Continue uphill past the nursery.

The trail begins to level out at about 0.5 mile and enters a scattered oak forest. There are several different kinds of oak here, and you can have the children see how many different kinds of leaves and acorns they can find along the trail. Also have them see if they can tell the different kinds of oaks apart by the way their trunks grow. (Some are tall and straight while others have multiple trunks that bend into grotesque shapes.) In the spring you can have them see if they can find different kinds of wildflowers beneath the trees than those they have seen along the open sections of the trail. There are also some California buckeye along this section of trail.

At just under 0.8 mile you come to a gate and fence. Be sure to keep the gate closed. Just past the fence the trail forks. Take a right and stay on the Diablo View Trail as you follow the contour of the hill above a fairly steep ravine to your left. The trail continues through alternating open grassland and oak forest until the Diablo View Trail dead ends into the Spengler Trail at 1.25 miles.

Take a right on the Spengler Trail as it heads downhill. At about 1.4 miles there is a gate across the trail, and a hikers' gate above it. Use the hikers' gate and remember to latch it so that the cattle do not get into grazing land they are not supposed to.

The trail is shaded by overhanging oak along this section, and there are plenty of bird sounds here during the spring and summer. Have the children see how many different bird songs they can hear.

Just past 1.5 miles you cross Alhambra Creek and the Spengler Trail heads off to the left. Take a right onto Alhambra Creek Trail and head down the fire road as it follows Alhambra Creek downhill. There is a small foot trail that follows close to the banks of the creek and the children may have more fun following it. The fire road is an easier hike, and is preferable if the ground is wet and muddy.

After 1.6 miles the creek drops down away from both the foot trail and fire road. During the summer you can actually hike down the creek itself because the water is very low, if present at all, along this stretch.

Wild grapes can be seen growing in the trees along the Alhambra Creek Trail here, and the children can taste the tart, purple grapes after they get ripe.

Broad trails offer plenty of space for both hikers and equestrians in Contra Costa County parks.

Between 1.5 and 1.9 miles there are several spur trails that lead down to the creek, where you can take a break, eat lunch, and let the children play among the rocks.

Wildflowers can be found along this shaded stretch of trail late into the summer, although they are not as brilliant or bountiful as they are during the spectacular spring bloom. The summer blooms tend to be smaller, and are often hidden by low-lying scrub. Children are delighted when they find blooming plants in the undergrowth after the ones in the more open areas are all gone.

The fire road returns to the edge of the creek between 2 and 2.5 miles, and the creek banks are easily accessible. Just before 2.5 miles a feeder creek crosses under the fire road through a culvert, and a grove of fifteen to twenty California buckeye grow alongside it before it reaches the more dense growth along Alhambra Creek. Have the children look for the buckeye seeds here. The buckeye seed is the largest tree seed found in North America, and children like to feel their smooth covering.

Just past 2.5 miles the trail passes by two huge buckeye trees that grow near the creek, and reaches the developed picnic area on the left. You can stop here for lunch or continue over the creek to return to the parking area at 3 miles.

---

45. Chamise/Mahogany/Trapline/ Gooseberry Trails Loop

Type: Dayhike
Difficulty: Moderate to difficult for children
Distance: 3 miles, loop
Hiking time: 2 hours
Elevation gain: 600 feet
Hikable: Year-round
Map: East Bay Regional Park

Las Trampas Regional Wilderness is a true urban wilderness area, sitting between heavily populated East Bay cities and the bedroom communities of Contra Costa County. Although the countryside surrounding the wilderness area is highly developed, the 3,618 acres within it are completely undeveloped except for a single parking lot at the end of Bollinger Canyon Road and an excellent trail system.

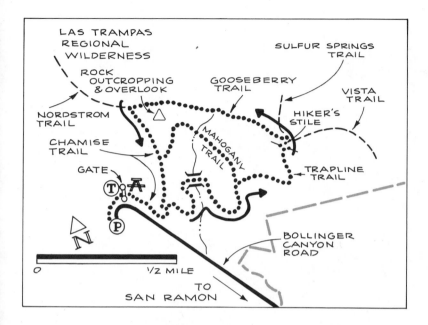

LAS TRAMPAS
REGIONAL
WILDERNESS

SULFUR SPRINGS
TRAIL

ROCK
OUTCROPPING
& OVERLOOK

GOOSEBERRY
TRAIL

VISTA
TRAIL

NORDSTROM
TRAIL

HIKER'S
STILE

CHAMISE
TRAIL

MAHOGANY
TRAIL

GATE

TRAPLINE
TRAIL

N

BOLLINGER
CANYON
ROAD

0   1/2 MILE

TO
SAN RAMON

Bollinger Creek bisects the park, with Rocky Ridge to the southwest and Las Trampas Ridge to the northeast. Two major earthquake faults—Las Trampas and Bollinger—are the origin of the uplifts that expose four well-defined geological formations within the wilderness area. The dominant vegetation on the southern and western exposures of the ridges is a dense chaparral with black sage, chamise, and buckbrush that is interspersed with toyon, manzanita, and other low-lying plants. Coast live oak, bay, and buckeye are the dominant trees found in the area, although several other oaks also grow here. Birds, particularly large raptors (including golden eagles), and small mammals are abundant in the region.

From I-680 near San Ramon, take Crow Canyon Road west to Bollinger Canyon Road. Continue northwest on it until it dead ends at the wilderness area parking lot.

From the parking lot, return to the end of Bollinger Canyon Road, and go through a gate to the trailhead for Chamise and Valley trails. Follow the Chamise Trail as it heads uphill for about 50 feet where you turn right and go through another gate. The trail winds around the contour of the hillside through open grassland.

Several large buckeye trees, which have beautiful large flower groups in the spring that turn into the largest seed of any tree in North America by midsummer, stand along this section of trail. After about 200 yards the trail drops down into a small ravine that has several types of oak and several more large buckeye. Near the road,

This gnarled oak has limbs for both climbing and sitting.

as the trail begins to climb out of the ravine, there is a picnic area underneath a large, spreading oak.

Follow the Chamise Trail up the hillside through open grassland. Have the children look for lizards and trapdoor spiders in the many holes alongside the trail. There are rattlesnakes in the area, so have the children beware of them.

At just past 0.5 mile the trail reaches a ridge where there is a grove of oak and a thicket of chaparral. The Chamise Trail leads off to the left and the Mahogany Trail leads to the right. Take the Mahogany Trail as it heads downhill. Just past the trail junction there is a good rest stop with a low-lying oak where the children can climb.

The Mahogany Trail begins a steep descent down the side of the hill through chaparral and bay. Have the children discuss why there are so many trunks on the bay trees (probably because the growth tip was damaged by grazing animals or storms).

Just before 0.75 mile the trail enters shade and you look down upon a slow-moving creek during the summer and fall that becomes a roaring torrent after the heavy winter rains. You are still 20 feet or so above the creek, but some trails lead down to the water. The children can head down these to explore the creekbed, or they can wait until the wooden footbridge that crosses the creek at just past 0.75 mile.

The trail begins to climb after it crosses the creek, and just before 1 mile it forks. The Mahogany Trail leads to the left, and descends back toward the creek. If the children are tired, you can take the Mahogany Trail back to the Chamise Trail for a 1.75-mile loop. For the hike described here, however, take the Trapline Trail to the right as it continues uphill.

There are plenty of wildflowers along this section of trail during the spring. Just past 1 mile there is a good example of adobe soil that has large cracks as it dries out during the summer.

As you reach a barbed wire fence, the trail leads back to the left, and at 1.2 miles the trail comes to a large stand of chaparral where large granite outcroppings can be seen on the hillsides. There are generally plenty of signs of bobcat and coyote along this section of the trail and the children can often spot their tracks on the open trail, especially after a rain.

At about 1.25 miles there is a good stopping point where a large oak gives good shade, and you can have a snack as you look out over distant ridges.

At about 1.5 miles the trail crosses a hikers' stile and reaches the ridge crest. It crosses the ridge, and comes to an open grassland area with large oaks where there is an excellent view of Mount Diablo to the east.

There is a trail junction about 100 feet past the stile. The Trapline Trail ends as the Sulfur Springs Trail goes straight ahead. The Gooseberry Trail goes to the left and the Vista Trail goes to the right. Take a left on the Gooseberry Trail as it heads along the top of the ridge. The views along this section of the trail are great—you can see the delta and Sacramento Valley to the east, and the East Bay Hills to the west.

At about 2.2 miles a spur trail leads out to a rock outcropping that overlooks Rocky Ridge to the west.

At 2.5 miles there is a trail junction. The Nordstrom Trail leads off to the right, and the Chamise Trail leads downhill to the left. Take the Chamise Trail to the left. During the early summer there are numerous salsify seed heads, which are similar to dandelion heads but much larger, along the trail in the grass. Have the children blow on one of these to see how the seeds are dispersed by the wind.

At 2.75 miles you return to the junction of the Chamise and Mahogany trails. You can take a breather here before heading back downhill. Just before 3 miles you return to the picnic area beside the road. You can return to the parking lot the way you came, or you can go through the gate and walk along the road to the parking area.

46. Fire Interpretive Trail

Type: Dayhike
Difficulty: Easy for children
Distance: 0.75 mile, loop
Hiking time: 1 hour
Elevation gain: None
Hikable: Year-round
Map: Mount Diablo Interpretive
Association

Mount Diablo State Park is a magnificent viewing platform that sits in the midst of an ever-expanding suburban development. It rises above the surrounding countryside where its California Coast Range environment is protected for all to enjoy, and those who hike its peaks and slopes can look out over the hills of Contra Costa and Alameda counties to the west and the Sacramento Valley to the east. On clear days the Sierra Nevada stand high against the eastern horizon, and during the winter the snow-covered western slopes of the Sierra stand out as a crisp reminder that real winter is a very short distance away. The Fire Interpretive Trail offers some of the best views of any available in the park as it circles the 3,849-foot summit.

From I-80, take I-680 south to either Walnut Creek or Danville. To reach the park from the north, from Walnut Creek take Ygnacio Valley Road east to North Gate Road; turn south on North Gate Road and continue to the park entrance. To reach the park from the south, from Danville take Diablo Road east to Diablo Scenic Boulevard; head north on Diablo Scenic Boulevard to the park entrance.

Enter the park from either the north or south entrance, and continue to Summit Road and the parking lot at the summit. Park at the lot downhill from the top of the summit. The Fire Interpretive Trail begins on the left about 50 yards back uphill toward the summit.

The first section of the trail leads through a canopy of oak and chaparral, and is paved for wheelchair and stroller access. The views from here are of the Sacramento/San Joaquin Delta, Suisun Bay, and the hills of northern Contra Costa County.

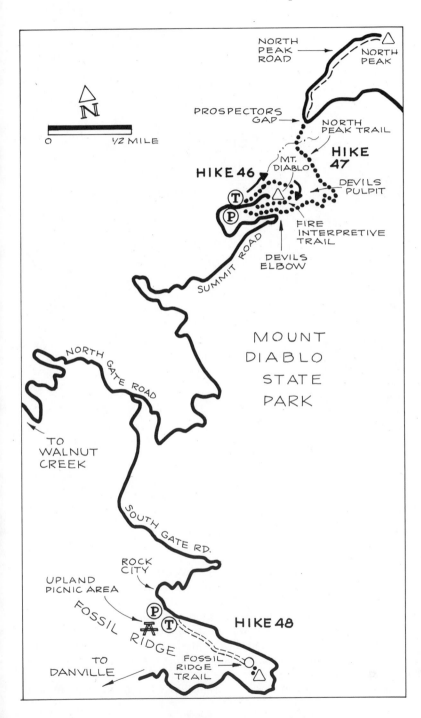

There is handicapped access on the interpretive trail around Mount Diablo.

At about 0.3 mile there is a large outcropping of Franciscan chert, and just past this outcropping the trail widens and has some benches where you can sit and look out over the countryside.

Ransome Point is about 50 feet past the overlook, and the trail turns to gravel here. It follows around the tip of the ridge and comes to another large outcropping of chert at about 0.5 mile at Devils Pulpit.

e Have the children look for signs of fires that have swept the ridge periodically, including a huge one in 1977 that denuded the slopes of the peak. They can look for various stages of growth that indicate fires from different times, and can see that the plant communities do regenerate after even the most fearsome fires.

You return to the parking lot at 0.75 mile.

---

47. North Peak Trail

Type: Dayhike
Difficulty: Moderate to difficult for children
Distance: 2.5 miles, round trip
Hiking time: 2 hours
Elevation gain: 600 feet
Hikable: Year-round
Map: Mount Diablo Interpretive Association

While the Fire Interpretive Trail around the summit of Mount Diablo offers a good overview of the countryside surrounding Mount Diablo, the hike down the slope of the peak to Prospectors Gap takes you through open grassland and thick chaparral to the gap between Mount Diablo and North Peak. This hike is excellent during the spring when wildflowers cover the slopes above and below the trail, and add a vibrant display of color to the green slopes between February and June. The views to the south of Mount Diablo are breathtaking as you climb out onto rock outcroppings at various sites, including the one just below Devils Pulpit.

Follow the directions to hike 46, Fire Interpretive Trail (map on page 161); park in the lower parking lot near the summit. The trailhead is on the right about 50 yards uphill from the parking lot.

The trail heads downhill on a moderate slope as it leads through a thick growth of chaparral. Have the children look at the various plants that grow along here and see if they can recognize some of the characteristics of chaparral (hard, stiff, small leaves and plants that have multiple trunks with good growth to protect the root systems from direct sun) and see how many different plants here have these characteristics.

At 0.25 mile the trail nears the paved road to the summit at Devils Elbow, and takes a sharp left turn as it continues downhill.

By 0.3 mile the chaparral cover has passed, and the trail heads through open grassland with only an occasional chaparral shrub or pine tree to offer shade.

At about 0.5 mile, directly below the large rock outcropping above the trail known as Devils Pulpit, the ridge juts out past the trail to a smaller rock outcropping. This is an excellent place to take a short rest and look out over the hills to the north of Mount Diablo. Be cautious of rattlesnakes, especially on warm fall or spring days when it has been cool at night. Rattlers like to soak up the warm sun on such days, and the rocks here are an ideal spot to do that.

Shortly after the stop, the trail curves to the left as it continues on a gentle slope downhill around the summit.

By 0.6 mile you reenter a canopy of chaparral, pine, and oak as the trail heads toward Prospectors Gap. The children can look for different types of oaks on the side of the trail along this stretch, and see how many wildflowers they can find in among the low-lying chaparral during the blooming season between February and June.

Just past 0.75 mile you cross a seasonal stream that drains the east slope of the mountain. Have the children look at the many different types of plants and shrubs that grow in this drainage area, and they can explore along the banks of the creek when there is water flowing.

The lookout on top of Mount Diablo gains prominence when viewed from below.

From the creek the trail continues through chaparral growth until about 1 mile, where you reach some open grassland with larger oak trees scattered about.

At 1.25 miles you reach Prospectors Gap, where the trail intersects a fire road that heads uphill to the top of North Peak. On the hike described here, you take a rest and lunch break at Prospectors Gap before heading back to the trailhead for a round trip of 2.5 miles.

If your party has enough energy, you can climb the additional 1.25 miles on the fire road to the top of North Peak, returning by the same route for a 5-mile round trip.

48. Artist Point/Fossil Ridge Trail

Type:	Dayhike
Difficulty:	Easy for children
Distance:	1.25 miles, round trip
Hiking time:	1 hour
Elevation gain:	200 feet
Hikable:	Year-round
Map:	Mount Diablo Interpretive Association

While the views from near the summit of Mount Diablo are magnificent and expansive, those from trails lower down on the slopes are intimate and comfortable. On the southwest side of the park, there are several trails that lead through open grasslands and oak woodlands that offer good views of some outstanding rock formations, the San Ramon Valley, and Las Trampas Ridge to the west. This is also an excellent area for viewing the early wildflower bloom after heavy winter rains. The trail to Fossil Ridge passes above the remnants of a devastating forest fire that burned about 2,500 acres at the base and on the slopes of Blackhawk Ridge in 1981. Above the trail lies Fossil Ridge, which is a hogback, or outcropping of rock, that runs the length of the ridge.

From I-80, take I-680 south to Danville and the Diablo Road exit. Follow Diablo Road east; it becomes Mount Diablo Scenic Drive and finally South Gate Road. Follow South Gate Road to the Uplands Picnic Area near Rock City Campground. Park in the small parking lot at the picnic area. (See map on page 161.)

The trail begins at the south side of the picnic area, heading uphill on an old, paved road. The road is not maintained, but is easily

Even the most ardent hikers sometimes leave the trail for trophies such as this salmon.

hiked as it leads uphill on a steep grade toward a stand of oaks. This north slope is covered by several types of oak, and the children can try to identify them (or at least make distinctions between the different species) by looking at their leaves and acorns. The different species also have different types of trunk growth.

At about 0.25 mile the trail reaches the ridge and levels out to a more gentle climb along the edge of the ridge. The oaks thin out along this stretch, and give way to open grassland where there is frequently a profuse wildflower bloom between February and June, particularly after heavy winter rains. Have the children keep an eye out for small flowers among the grass that they might overlook without searching for them. Although these flowers do not stand out as much as many of the more colorful, larger ones do, they are fascinating and children like to investigate their blooms through hand lenses and magnifying glasses.

The trail continues along the ridge as a wide fire road, and at a gentle grade, until about 0.6 mile, where the fire road ends in a turnaround. From here you take a single-track trail up the steep slope to the top of Fossil Ridge, where you can see out over San Ramon Valley and the children can explore among the rocks of the hogback. Have them be cautious of rattlesnakes; rock formations such as these are favorite spots for these reclusive animals.

Return to the parking area by the same route.

49. Black Point Trail

Type: Dayhike
Difficulty: Difficult for children
Distance: 4 miles, loop
Hiking time: 4 hours
Elevation gain: 1,000 feet
Hikable: Year-round
Map: Mount Diablo Interpretive Association

Mount Diablo stands above the surrounding countryside, and is an island of preserved natural communities among the heavily populated areas of Contra Costa County. As with many isolated islands, the park that extends from the valleys and flatlands surrounding it includes a wide variety of natural habitats and geological formations.

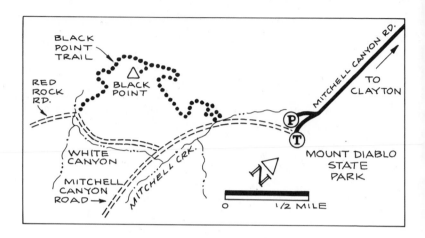

From land that lies below 1,000 feet in elevation to the summit at 3,849 feet, the range and diversity of habitats offer hikers great choices about where to go and what to observe. Many regions of the park have spectacular displays of color during the wildflower season that extends from February to June of each year, but the cooler north slope, which also happens to be more lightly used than the central ridges and southern slope, offers some of the best displays found in the region. A walk along the trails here takes you through areas covered with bright blossoms of more than a dozen species of wildflowers, including one found only on and around Mount Diablo. The Mount Diablo globe lily is a low-growing yellow flower with a blossom shaped like a small lantern, and is endemic to the region.

 From I-80, take I-680 south to the Clayton Road exit. Take Clayton Road south to Clayton; turn south on Mitchell Canyon Road and continue until the road dead ends at the day-use parking area. Park here, and begin the hike by following the Mitchell Canyon fire road south from the parking area.

The first mile of the hike leads along the open and level fire road. During and after the rainy season the children can explore along Mitchell Creek that runs along the west side of the road. The creek is often dry during summer and fall, but becomes a roaring torrent during heavy rains. When it is high and running swiftly, caution the children about playing in the water.

If you are taking the hike during the wildflower bloom, you will see many colorful blossoms among the emerald-green grass carpet on the side of the trail.

At about 1 mile turn right on Red Road as it winds up White Canyon. Watch for birds and other small animals along the creekbanks as you climb about 200 feet up the canyon. The slopes will be alive with color during the wildflower season, and the children might have

These girls are waiting for their laggard parents to catch up.

fun seeing how many different colors they can see, or how many different flowers of each color.

At 1.75 miles the lightly used Black Point Trail leads to the right. The sign marking the trail is small and not easily seen, so look carefully, because this is the trail you should take.

Between 1.75 and 2 miles the trail climbs steadily about 400 feet toward the ridge, and quickly climbs another 400 feet in about 200 yards. This is the rough section of the climb, but the rewards are great. As you reach the ridge, panoramic vistas open up, and the trail levels out.

At about 2.25 miles a short spur trail leads off to the right to the top of Black Point. Take this side trip of about 100 yards or so to the peak, where you can take a lunch and rest break. The children can keep an eye out for large birds soaring overhead. The black birds that fly with their wings in an upward V are vultures, and others that keep their wings flat as they soar are hawks of various types (mostly redtail). If you are lucky you may even spot a golden eagle soaring high above all other birds.

Return to the main trail after your break and take a right to continue along the ridge, which leads through a wonderland of wild-flowers during the spring bloom, until it heads downhill just before 2.5 miles.

After a short, steep descent the trail winds to the right around the contour of the slope before heading down a ridge. This is another excellent wildflower stretch, and the children can look for some of the many minute wildflowers that grow close to the ground on the hill-side. Have them use a magnifying glass or hand lens to examine these small jewels.

The trail takes a sharp left around the hill at about 3 miles and dead ends at the Mitchell Canyon fire road at about 3.5 miles.

Take a left and return to the parking area for a 4-mile round trip.

50. Nortonville/Black Diamond Trails Loop

Type: Dayhike
Difficulty: Moderate for children
Distance: 2.5 miles, loop
Hiking time: 2 hours
Elevation gain: 300 feet
Hikable: Year-round
Map: East Bay Regional Park District

The first land for 3,700-acre Black Diamond Mines Regional Preserve was acquired by the East Bay Regional Parks District in the 1970s, and today it is an outstanding historical park that documents the early coal mining in the region as well as an ideal hiking and

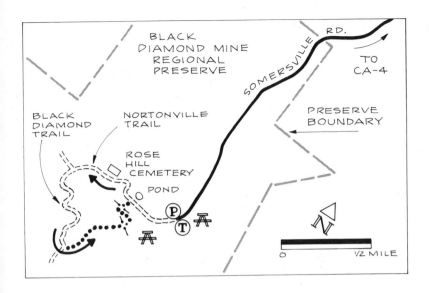

nature study area. Native Americans lived in the area for thousands of years before the arrival of Europeans in the late 1700s, but the natives and their villages were rapidly destroyed by that contact. By the 1860s coal mining replaced ranching in the area, and this lasted until after the turn of the century. Although little remains of the many small communities that thrived in the region during coal mining times, a cemetery on a hillside above the old mines serves as a monument to the residents who lived here, and an examination of the tombstones in the cemetery gives everyone an idea of what life must have been like in those bygone days. The 34 miles of trails within the park traverse some of the most spectacular wildflower displays in the region during the spring, and there is a wide variety of flora and fauna within the park, including some plants found nowhere else in the region.

From I-80, take I-680 and then CA-4 east. Take the Somersville Road exit and go south on Somersville Road until it dead ends in the park. The trailhead is at the southern end of the parking area.

Follow the signs to Cemetery and Nortonville Trail to the right. The trail begins a gentle climb as it heads toward the cemetery through open grassland with an occasional oak. At 0.1 mile and again at 0.2 mile the trail forks; stay right at each fork. At about 0.2 mile there is a large grove of young California buckeye. This migrant from more tropical climates has the largest seed of any tree in North America, and is unusual among deciduous trees of these regions in that it goes into dormancy during early summer when the first severe heat arrives. It drops its leaves then, and stays dormant until the next spring.

Children like to search for and play with the hard, shiny brown seeds in the fall after they have fallen from the trees.

At 0.25 mile you pass through an open gate and on the right is a small pond that is home to frogs, tadpoles, and other small water animals. This pond sometimes dries up during late summer, but in most years there is water in it year-round.

Just before 0.5 mile you come to a trail on the right that leads to the old cemetery. Take this side trail and spend some time reading the old tombstones to get a sense of history about the region. Talk with the children about why so many young children died in those days, and also about the high mortality rate among miners.

The side trail heads out of the rear of the cemetery and rejoins

Human history can often be found in trailside sites such as this cemetery on the slopes of Black Diamond Mines Regional Park.

the main trail at just past 0.5 mile. Continue uphill on Nortonville Trail as it heads through open grasslands that are dotted with brilliant displays of wildflowers during the spring. Have the children look for the many small flowers that grow low to the ground in the grass. They can examine these through a hand lens to see their dainty characteristics. During the summer and fall, children can look for the many different seed pods that form after the blooms have gone.

The Nortonville Trail leads under large power lines at 1 mile, and the Black Diamond Trail leads off to the left just before the power lines. Take the Black Diamond Trail as it levels out and follows the contour of the hill. The trail provides outstanding vistas as it leads in and out of stands of oak until about 1.5 miles. The children can look at the different types of leaves on the various oaks. There are plenty of young oak along this stretch of trail, and you can talk to the children about how these provide browse for deer, and have them look for signs of deer prints and where they may have been browsing on some of the young oak.

At 1.5 miles the Black Diamond Trail turns to the right and leads downhill, and a single-track trail leads straight ahead down the ridge. Take the unnamed trail leading straight ahead.

The trail runs alongside a barbed wire fence on this section of the trail. The views here include several of old mine sites. Have the children look for unusual color formations that stand out against the natural browns and greens to find the piles of debris that were left over from the mines.

The trail takes a rather straight path downhill here; caution the children about running, because they may fall into the barbed wire, which can be very painful.

At about 1.7 miles there is an old tree that has fallen across the trail, and this is a good spot for the children to climb, play, and explore how small insects and animals use the decaying tree for food and shelter. Mention how it is important to leave some decaying trees for just this reason.

At 1.8 miles you come to a hikers' stile at the end of the trail, after about 50 feet of steep descent where you have to be careful not to slip and slide down the hill. Do not go through the stile, but take a left to continue down the hill toward Nortonville Trail. This takes you back into the large grove of California buckeye, and the children can look for the hard, shiny brown seed pods.

The trail curves to lead parallel to the Nortonville Trail, but slightly above it. At 2 miles you go through another hikers' stile and after about another 100 yards the trail joins the Nortonville Trail. Continue back toward the parking lot, and at about 2.25 miles there is a large picnic area to the right. This is a good spot to have a rest and lunch before returning to the car at 2.5 miles.

51. Ridge Trail

Type: Dayhike
Difficulty: Moderate for children
Distance: 2 miles, round trip
Hiking time: 2 hours
Elevation gain: 300 feet
Hikable: Year-round
Map: East Bay Regional Park District

Contra Loma Regional Park is a 776-acre oasis in the midst of suburban Antioch that offers a number of attractions to hikers and families. Both swimming and fishing are done in the lake, and windsurfing has become increasingly popular. The hills above the lake are open grassland, and several of the trails connect with those in the adjoining Black Diamond Mines Regional Preserve. These are particularly popular with equestrians, but several trails limited to Contra Loma Regional Park are very popular with families during the cool days of fall, winter, and spring when the warm rays of the low

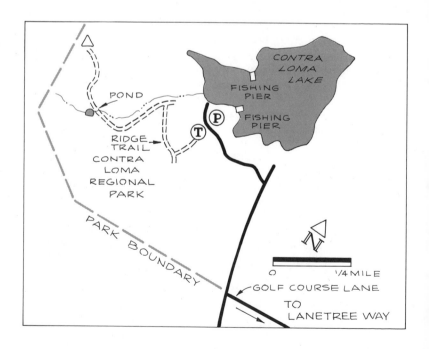

Many parks have views of man-made and natural lakes.

sun make them ideal outings. This entire hike leads through vast blooms of wildflowers from February to June, especially after wet years.

Take I-80 and I-680 to CA-4. Head east to Antioch. In Antioch, take Lone Tree Way south off CA-4 to Golf Course Lane. Take a right and follow the signs to the park. Continue past the kiosk to the westernmost parking lot.

Follow the equestrian trail signs uphill to the equestrian staging area behind the overflow parking area. Go through the gate and follow the single-track trail uphill along the fence line.

The trail leads over open grassland until 0.25 mile, where the single-track trail dead ends at a wide horse trail. Take a right here as the trail winds around the contour of the hills above the lake. There are excellent views of Antioch, the lower delta, and the coastal hills to the north from here.

By 0.5 mile you are above the park headquarters, and you pass by several small rock outcroppings where the children can keep an eye out for lizards and snakes. Caution them about rattlesnakes; they are found in the park during much of the year.

Just past 0.5 mile the trail drops down toward a seasonal creek and dead ends at a T intersection. Take a left to head uphill for the continuation of the hike. (Take a right, and another right at the next junction, if you wish to head for the lake.)

There is a large cottonwood beside the creek on the right side of the road about 50 feet uphill. The children may explore along the creekbed when it is dry, or along the water's edge when it is flowing.

At 0.75 mile the road curves to the right and forms a dam over the creek. During wet years this pond has some water year-round, and is home to tadpoles, frogs, and other small animals and insects. The children can explore around the edges of the pond in search of these.

As the road continues uphill past the pond, there are several areas with large outcroppings of rock. These are volcanic in origin, and you can talk to the children about how the rocks were formed, and see if they can observe how the outcroppings form the top of the ridge. This becomes more obvious as you approach the top of the hill.

At 1 mile the road ends, and there is a good picnic spot at the tip of the ridge where you can look out over the lake, Antioch, and the lower delta as you eat.

Return to the parking area by the same route, or take the shortcut to the lake, described earlier.

52. Highland/Coyote Trails Loop

Type: Dayhike
Difficulty: Moderate for children
Distance: 1.5 miles, loop
Hiking time: 2 hours
Elevation gain: 100 feet
Hikable: Year-round
Map: East Bay Regional Park District

Morgan Territory Regional Preserve is a real wilderness near one of the most populated areas in the state. This little-used preserve was once home to one of the five Native American groups in the Diablo area, and was then a large ranch for the last half of the nineteenth century. Today it is home to more than ninety species of wildflowers, including the Diablo sunflower—which grows only in the foothills of Mount Diablo—as well as deer, coyote, and even mountain lion. Hikes can take you through oak and bay forests or to the top of ridges that offer expansive vistas that extend all the way to the Sierra Nevada to the east. One word of caution about hiking in this preserve. I found the map provided by East Bay Regional Park District difficult to use.

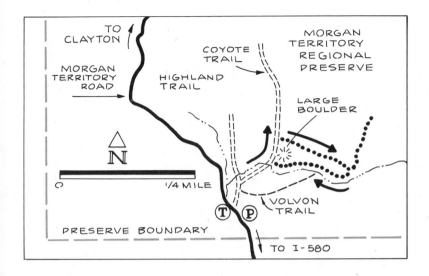

Either I could not locate the trailhead that I was looking for, or the trails that led from there had been changed drastically since the map was made. You may wish to check out the routes of the trails on the map with park rangers before heading out.

From the north, follow directions to Clayton given in hike 49, Black Point Trail; from Clayton, take Highland Road to Morgan Territory Road and head for the Highland trailhead about 2 miles north of the park headquarters near the south end of the preserve. From the south, take I-5 south to I-205 and I-580 east to Livermore; take Marsh Creek Road north to Morgan Territory Road, and park at the south end of the preserve.

Take the Highland Trail to the east from Morgan Territory Road as it leads along a seasonal creek with a mixed stand of oak, California bay, toyon, and broad-leaf maple on the hillside.

The children can search for the fruit of the bay tree in late summer and early fall. This fruit looks like a small avocado (about the size of a large thumb) and was used as a food by Native Americans in the region. You can taste these if you find them, but you'll probably find them too bitter for the modern palate.

At 0.1 mile the trail forks. The Highland Trail leads left, the Coyote Trail leads straight ahead, and the Volvon Trail goes off to the right. Take the trail straight ahead to head up the Coyote Trail as it follows another seasonal creek.

The trail leads under a canopy of oak and bay on a level fire road. There are some wild grapes along the trail here, and the children will want to taste them as they ripen in late summer and early fall.

Just past 0.25 mile the trail turns to the left and crosses over

Keep an eye on the trail for small animal life such as this lizard.

the creek where there are some pools of water even at the end of dry summers. There is easy access here, and a large boulder to climb on, but you will be returning here near the end of the hike, so the children may want to wait to explore the area.

The trail begins an uphill climb past the creek. This stretch is primarily open grassland where you can keep an eye out for signs of coyote, rodents in the meadows, and hawks and vultures soaring overhead. This section also is full of colorful wildflowers during the spring bloom.

At 0.5 mile a single-track trail leads off to the right across another open meadow. The signs say both this and the trail you are on are the Coyote Trail. For an optional side trip, stay left and continue uphill on the fire road—the trail you were on—and you come to a drainage area at about 0.6 mile where the children can climb on some rock outcroppings as you rest and eat.

For the hike described here, take a right on the single-track trail to head across the meadow. Watch for signs of coyote here, and see if there are any raptors (hawks and vultures) soaring overhead.

At about 0.75 mile the trail enters a cover of oak and bay, and after another 200 yards curves to follow a creek upstream. This creek is the one that Coyote Trail crossed at 0.25 mile. Instead of following the trail, head down to the creek.

If the creek is dry, you can simply head down the creekbed to the right. If it has water in it, you can walk along the animal paths on the hillside above the creek.

As you hike either in or above the creek, you will see plenty of signs of wildlife. Deer, raccoon, and coyote are all numerous in the park, as well as many small birds.

At just past 1 mile you return to the Coyote Trail fire road. This is where the standing pond and large boulder are located, and this is an excellent place to stop for a rest and picnic.

Return to the parking area by the same route to complete a 1.25-mile loop.

53. River of Skulls Nature Trail

Type: Dayhike
Difficulty: Easy for children
Distance: 1 mile, loop
Hiking time: 1 hour
Elevation gain: 100 feet
Hikable: Year-round
Map: US Army Corps of Engineers

The first European explorers to pass through the region where New Hogan Lake lies were probably Jedediah Smith and his party of trappers, who were reputed to have passed through the region in 1827, but there are stories that the native Miwok called the river here a Spanish name, Calaveras (which means "river of skulls"), in 1836, so there is some dispute over who was first. What is undisputed is that the Miwok lived in the region for several thousand years before the Europeans came, living off the land. There was plentiful food here. The oak supplied an almost unending supply of acorns, deer and small game such as squirrel and rabbit roamed the open grasslands on the slopes, and salmon were plentiful in the undammed river. Although there is no doubt that Europeans had settled in the region by the 1840s, it wasn't until the tremendous influx of miners after gold was

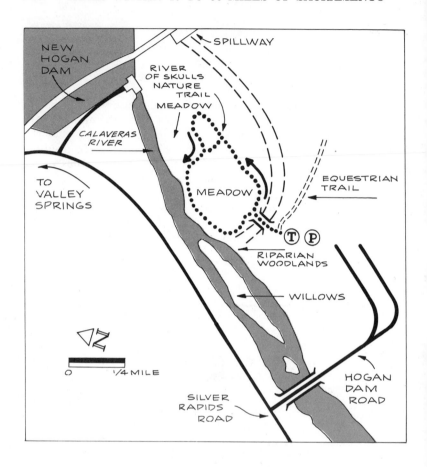

discovered that the life of the Miwok was changed for the worse. Today there is little sign of the Miwok other than an occasional bedrock mortar or small grinding stone. In fact, there is little more reminder of the gold miners who flocked to the region in the 1850s. Many of their small towns are now inundated by the waters of the lake, and only tales remain of their wild and woolly existence. The flora and fauna of the region has changed little since the early days of the Miwok, though, and the self-guided nature trail below the dam is an excellent introduction to the plants and how they were used by the Miwok. You can pick up a booklet at the park headquarters on Hogan Dam Road on your way to the trail, or you can order one beforehand by calling or writing the US Army Corps of Engineers (New Hogan Lake, PO Box 128, Valley Springs, CA 95252; 209-772-1343).

 From CA-99 south, take CA-12 east to Valley Springs. Take CA-26 south to Hogan Dam Road just south of Valley Springs. Continue until Silver Rapids Road veers to the right; stay left on Hogan Dam Road and proceed to the left to the Monte Vista Parking Area immediately below the dam.

Take the nature trail to the left out of the rear of the parking area; the trail crosses the rock spillway on a wooden footbridge.

After crossing the bridge, take a right as the trail leads toward a grove of blue oak, where there are several benches at about 0.25 mile. Have the children try to locate some of the acorns from these oaks, which were a favorite food of the Miwok.

From the grove of blue oak the trail begins a slow uphill climb through a thick growth of chaparral. Use the interpretive booklet to have the children find *yerba santa*, chamise, and buckbrush among the shrubs at about 0.3 mile. They may also want to identify poison oak here if they don't know what it looks like.

From about 0.3 mile to 0.5 mile, the trail is generally level and passes by some digger pines, the only pine tree native to the foothill woodlands. These trees furnished food to the Miwok, because the pine nuts from them were rich in food value and highly prized. The Miwok

Deer keep a wary eye on intruders in their browsing areas.

also used the bark from the trees to build shelters.

Manzanita and toyon, two chaparral plants that provided berries for the natives, are also found along here. The manzanita bush has a dark reddish-brown bark that peels off in curlicues. The children like to play with these when they find them on the ground.

The trail heads downhill at about 0.5 mile and there are several types of oak along here. See if the children can find the black oak, valley oak, and interior live oak.

The trail takes a sharp left turn at about 0.6 mile (you can continue straight ahead for a 0.3-mile loop side trip), leads past several large oaks, and comes to some California buckeye on the hillside above the trail. These tropical immigrants are very different from most deciduous trees of the region, because they go into dormancy at the first real heat of summer and stay dormant until the next spring. During the spring they have bunches of white flowers that turn into the largest seed of any tree in North America. Children like to hunt for these large, smooth, brown seeds in the late summer and fall.

The trail heads to the Calaveras River at about 0.75 mile, and passes through an area of thick riparian growth that is filled with plants used in one way or another by the Miwok. Have the children use the interpretive booklet to find some of these.

You return to the parking area at 1 mile.

If you would like to take a little longer hike after completing this one, you can take the equestrian trail east out of the parking lot. This 3-mile-long trail follows the shoreline of New Hogan Lake through oak woodlands and open grasslands.

54. North/South Nature Trails Loop

Type: Dayhike
Difficulty: Moderate for children
Distance: 2 miles, loop
Hiking time: 2 hours
Elevation gain: 50 feet
Hikable: Year-round
Map: California State Park

Indian Grinding Rocks State Historic Park offers both excellent natural history and human history hikes. The park is nestled in a small valley with open meadows and large valley oaks at about 2,400

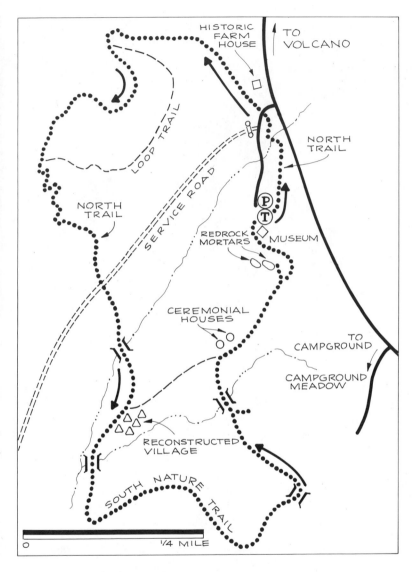

feet elevation. The central attraction of the 135-acre park is the outcropping of marbleized limestone that has more than 1,000 mortar holes in it. This is the largest collection of bedrock mortars found anywhere in the United States. The Miwok Indians, who used the mortars, lived along the banks of creeks and rivers in the northern Sierra Nevada, and the acorns from the large valley oaks provided a mainstay of their diet. The acorns were ground in the mortars in the park, and then used in a variety of ways. Gold miners and ranchers

Native Americans lived in the Sierra Nevada foothills long before Europeans settled here.

displaced the Miwok over most of their territory in the mid-1850s, including the valley where the park is located. The park has reconstructed a typical Miwok village in the meadow, and has a good museum that describes their way of life. The Miwok used many of the more than 130 species of plants found in the park, and the birds you can see and hear there were also familiar to the Miwok.

 From US 50, take CA-49 south to CA-88. Go east on CA-88 to Pine Grove, and take Pine Grove–Volcano Road north for 1.5 miles to the park entrance. Turn west into the park, and park near the museum. The North Trail begins near the front entrance of the museum.

The North Trail leads uphill from the parking lot in front of the museum, and heads through a covering of oak and pine. It follows the contour of the hill back toward the entrance to the park, crosses over a seasonal creek at about 0.15 mile, and then almost immediately crosses over the entrance road to the park.

Continue uphill through open grassland with some manzanita. This is one of the most widespread chaparral plants found in the Sierra Nevada foothills, and it is easily recognizable by its smooth red-brown bark. *Manzanita* means "small apple" in Spanish, and was named by the early Spanish explorers, who thought that was what its small fruit resembled. Both the Native Americans in the region and the early explorers used the fruit as food.

At about 0.3 mile, after a gentle climb, the trail reaches a large valley oak near the fence that sits on the park boundary. You can stop here and look back over the meadow below, and the old farmhouse that sits near the park entrance.

Take a sharp left on the trail and head back uphill for about 100 yards to a trail junction. You can take either trail here (the left-hand is the Loop Trail), but for this hike, veer to the right and head uphill into more chaparral and oak. There are several varieties of oaks in this grove, and the children can group them by the type of leaves they have, the shape of their trunks, and the type of acorns that fall to the ground.

There is plenty of coyote scat along this stretch of trail, and you can have the children search for footprints.

At 0.4 mile the trail begins a descent through a thicket of young manzanita. You pass the other end of the Loop Trail as it comes in from the left.

At about 0.6 mile the young manzanita give way to young oak, incense cedar, and pine. I would guess from the thick growth of all three that there was a forest fire here several decades ago that burned the hillside, and gave the seeds of these young plants a chance to grow.

At 0.9 mile the trail crosses a gravel road as it follows along the edge of a fragile meadow. Please stay out of the meadow; human traffic will destroy the habitat of many small animals.

By 1 mile you come to several large valley oak beside the trail. The children can look at these and explore around their bases as you discuss how the natives in the region depended upon trees such as these (and these were alive well before Europeans reached the region) for food and fuel.

You can also see how acorn woodpeckers have used the thick bark of the trees to store food for the winter.

Just before 1 mile the trail crosses a seasonal creek on a wooden footbridge. The children can explore around the creek here, and like to search along the banks when there is water flowing. There are many small birds that live in the riparian growth.

Just past 1 mile you come to a reconstructed village where the children like to explore and pretend they are Miwoks of earlier times.

You have the option of returning to the museum by taking the trail that heads left out of the village for a 1.5-mile loop, but this hike heads right on the self-guided South Nature Trail. You can either pick up a booklet for this trail at the museum or at the ceremonial round-house in the reconstructed Miwok village in the middle of the meadow.

After about 100 yards the trail crosses a wooden footbridge, where the children can explore along the creek if there is any water in it, and then heads uphill along the park boundary.

The trail follows along the upper contour of the hill and through a grove of young madrone trees. These appear to be about the same age as the young manzanita, pine, incense cedar, and oak on the North Trail.

As you pass through the grove of madrone you come to a large patch of mountain misery. This low-lying plant has fernlike leaves, and got its name because its sticky leaves adhere to anything that comes into contact with them. Early pioneers thought it was sheer misery to hike through large patches of it. Black bears are thought to eat large quantities of the plant just before they hibernate in the winter because it is not easily digested.

At the end of the patch of mountain misery, near 1.25 miles, there is a large incense cedar that has twin trunks, and a sheared-off top. Have the children guess how the tree got two trunks (probably because it stands in an area where there are high winds in the winter and the top keeps getting broken off).

The trail continues to curve around the hill and begins a slight descent until it crosses a small seasonal creek and then a larger seasonal creek on a bridge just before it comes to the practice house in the reconstructed Miwok village at 1.8 miles. The children can explore around the reconstructed round and practice houses, and then take the boardwalk out over the large bedrock mortar before returning to the museum at 2 miles.

55. Miwok Trail

Type: Dayhike
Difficulty: Easy for children
Distance: 0.5 mile, loop
Hiking time: 45 minutes
Elevation gain: 100 feet
Hikable: Year-round
Map: El Dorado Irrigation District

Sly Park Recreation Area has developed around Jenkinson Lake, which was formed by the construction of the Jenkinson Dam in the 1930s. It is an excellent introductory hiking area for families, particularly those with younger children. The recreation area also has a number of campgrounds for families who would like to stay over-

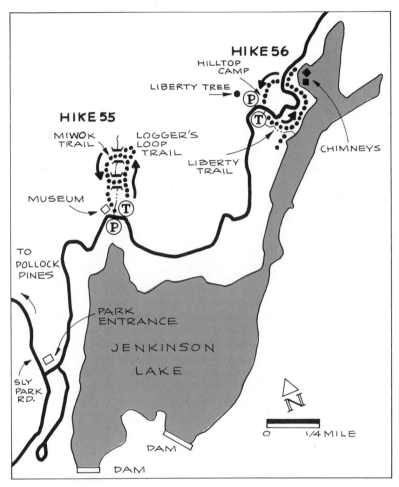

night in the area and hike for several days. The lake sits above a mountain gorge in a ponderosa pine forest with a wide variety of plants and animals. The recreation area is above the often-enervating heat of summer in the Sacramento Valley, and offers a welcome relief to families who come for a day or a week to hike around its shores. During summer weekends the area is crowded, but most visitors come to enjoy water sports such as fishing, boating, and swimming. The trails are often empty of hikers, and equestrians have their own trails.

Take US 50 east to Pollock Pines. Take Sly Park Road south from Pollock Pines and continue 5 miles to the park entrance. After entering the park, take a left turn and continue for about 0.75 mile to the James Calvin Sly Museum and Miwok Trail. Park on either side of the road near the museum.

Wooded hillsides and flowing streams are only a few of the attractions of the trails around Jenkinson Lake.

The Miwok Trail, a self-guided nature trail, begins at the museum, which is open on weekends only. You can pick up a brochure for this self-guiding nature trail at the museum or at the beginning of the trail near the wooden footbridge.

Head to the right on the trail. You first pass a well that is fed by a spring, and then cross a wooden footbridge after about 100 feet.

Among the trees marked along the trail is the Pacific yew, which was a little-known tree until taxol, a substance that is a potential cure for some cancers, was discovered in its bark.

The trail leads upstream, and at about 0.2 mile there is access to the creek near a footbridge. This is a good place to observe the creek when it is flowing in the winter and spring, or to explore along its banks when it is lower.

 For a shorter hike, you can cross the bridge here and return to the museum, but for the hike described here, take a right at the bridge and head uphill to continue the longer loop.

At about 0.25 mile the Loggers' Loop takes off to the right for a side trip. Follow this trail as it leads uphill past a large, downed incense cedar and an old stump with "loggers' notches" in it. These notches were made by early loggers so they could insert platforms to stand on as they felled the trees above the knotty bases.

Have the children imagine the problems early loggers had working in the dense forests. Ask if they can envision how the large logs were moved to sawmills. You might also check to see if the children know when the dam was built, and when that was in relation to the time the early loggers were clearing the surrounding slopes.

At about 0.35 mile you come to another footbridge that crosses over the creek as the trail takes a sharp left to return on the opposite side of the creek. A large fir and a large incense cedar rise above the creek near the bridge.

Follow the trail down the creek, which has several access points, to the museum at 0.5 mile.

---

56. Liberty/Chimney Trails Loop

Type: Dayhike
Difficulty: Moderate for children
Distance: 1.25 miles, loop
Hiking time: 1 hour
Elevation gain: 200 feet
Hikable: Year-round
Map: El Dorado Irrigation District

The short trail described before this one (see hike 55, Miwok Trail) introduces hikers to the many plants found around Jenkinson Lake in Sly Park Recreation Area. The trail described here, the longer Liberty Trail, is marked to identify many of the trees and plants described on the Miwok Trail, and leads out into the open grasslands around the shores of the lake where digger pine and chaparral plants, particularly manzanita, replace the pine, incense cedar, and fir that grow on the higher slopes. These two trails are only a small part of the trails that lead around the lake, however, and after taking them, many hikers want to expand their hikes. That is possible in this recreation area, with an 8-mile-long trail that circumnavigates the lake. With a combination of campgrounds where families can spend their nights and short and long trails that are relatively level, Sly Park Recreation Area is a pleasant destination for families who like to hike and also want to escape from the summer heat of the Sacramento Valley.

Follow directions given in the previous hike (see map on page 187) and continue for another 2 miles past the museum to the huge fir that has been designated the Liberty Tree. Park on the downhill side of the road from the Liberty Tree. Begin the hike by crossing the road to read about and explore around the base of this 200-foot-tall Douglas fir.

The Liberty Trail begins downhill from the parking area. Follow the trail down toward the marked nature trail. Signs along the trail identify many of the trees and small plants, and the trail guide from the Miwok Trail (see hike 55) gives information about many of them.

At about 0.1 mile the trail splits. Take a right here over a small footbridge. The trail continues down the side of the stream, where the children can explore.

At 0.3 mile the Liberty Trail ends in a T junction with a trail that curves along the shore of the lake. The creek enters the lake here, and the children can explore among the riparian plants that grow along the creek for small birds that use the trees for nesting and feeding. They can also explore along the shore of the lake here; the access is excellent.

After exploring along the creek and lakeshore, take a left on the shoreline trail toward Chimney Camp. The trail leaves the canopy of the tall trees and enters a stretch of grasslands and chaparral. The dominant chaparral plant along here is manzanita, a low-lying shrub with hard leaves and a shiny brown bark that peels off in layers during the year. Have the children feel the smooth, hard wood of the manzanita, and talk about how chaparral plants are hard and prickly, with a thick growth of branches to protect the roots and lower trunk from the heat of the summer sun. Mention that *manzanita* means "little apple" in Spanish, and that the Native Americans and early Spanish explorers used the small fruit of the plant for food and tea.

The trail leads around the ragged shoreline just above high water, and the children can search for tracks of raccoon, deer, and coyote that are frequently visible along the dirt trail.

Just before 0.5 mile you enter a canopy of oak and pine, and beneath the trees is a low-lying plant with fernlike leaves. This plant was known as mountain misery by early pioneers because its leaves are covered with a sticky substance and stick to objects such as boots and pants that come into contact with them. Mountain misery is thought to be a favorite food of black bears before they hibernate for the winter. It seems that the plant is difficult to digest, and stays in the bears' stomachs during the long hibernation. The children can

Look around forest debris for signs of wildlife such as this pack rat mound.

feel the plant to see how much misery it would be to hike through large patches of it.

At about 0.6 mile you reach a small inlet where several old chimneys rise above the water (or are completely exposed during low water). These are the remains of some old buildings that were inundated when the lake was formed.

The trail curves around the inlet, and at about 0.7 mile crosses the paved park road. There are numerous ground squirrels that scurry along this section of the trail. If the children are quiet, they may get quite close to some. Do not attempt to feed or handle them, however, because they are carriers of both plague and rabies.

After you cross the road, veer to the right as the trail heads uphill toward the Hill Top Campground. The trail crosses several long rows of large boulders that have obviously been placed along the hillside, probably for erosion control.

You reach the campground at about 0.8 mile. Cross a paved road to the sign that says HILLTOP TRAIL TO LAKE 0.2 MILE. Follow the trail downhill to a short spur trail at the 1-mile point. This short spur trail leads down to one of the lower footbridges on the Liberty Trail. Here, take a right and head back uphill to the parking area at 1.25 miles.

57. Big Trees Interpretive/Forest View Trails Loop

Type: Dayhike
Difficulty: Easy for children
Distance: 1.5 miles, loop
Hiking time: 2 hours
Elevation gain: Minimal
Hikable: Year-round
Map: US Forest Service

Located in Tahoe National Forest, the small Placer County Big Tree Grove of *Sequoiadendron giganteum,* or giant sequoia, is the northernmost grove in California, the only state in which they occur naturally. The nearest grove of these trees, the largest living things in the world, is at Calaveras Big Trees State Park, more than 60 miles south. While the grove at Calaveras Big Trees contains hundreds of these giants, the Placer County Big Tree Grove has only six live sequoia and two dead ones that are said to have fallen in the nineteenth century. This small grove was discovered by a gold prospector in 1855, and has been protected since 1892, when there was concern by local citizens that the trees might be cut for lumber. In 1990 the US Forest Service gave additional protection to the 160 acres surrounding the grove by designating it as a Botanical Area. The grove has been a popular attraction for well over a century, as attested to by the names and dates carved between 1860 and 1890 in some of the smooth-barked alders along the creek that runs through the grove. This was noted by a visitor in 1891. You may want to search for such inscriptions on the trees when you visit, although it is unlikely you will find any from the 1860s.

Take I-80 east to Foresthill and exit onto Mosquito Ridge Road (Forest Road 96). Continue 22 miles east from Foresthill, take Big Trees Road, and drive 1 mile to the grove. The trails begin at the parking lot.

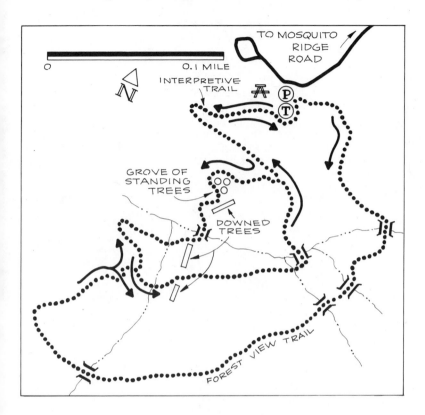

There are seventeen numbered stations along the 0.5-mile Big Trees Interpretive Trail that are described in the self-guiding brochure, available from the Foresthill Ranger District Office (USFS, 22830 Foresthill Road, Foresthill, CA 95631; 916-367-2224).

The trail winds among the six standing and two fallen sequoia trees, and you are cautioned to stay on the trail here, for heavy foot traffic near the base of the standing trees may cause damage.

The trail leads through an old-growth forest with four other species of conifers (cone-bearing trees) as well as several types of smaller shrubs and small broadleaf plants. Have the children read the information plaque at Station 1 as you start out, and then keep track of how many different trees and shrubs they can identify as you complete the hike.

At about 200 yards the trail forks. Take the trail to the right to follow the numbered stations in sequence.

The first four giant sequoias are located at Station 5 at about 300 yards and, at about 500 to 700 years old, are the youngest of the stand. Have the children compare the bark of the sequoia with that

Blossoms add bright colors that stand out against the dark understory of mountain forests.

of the fir and pine you have passed along the trail.

Just past Station 5 you come to a grove of young trees that were planted as seedlings in 1951, and then the first of the two fallen trees in the grove. This tree likely fell during a windstorm in 1861 or 1862. You can stand by the base of the tree to get an idea of its size.

The second fallen tree is at about 0.2 mile, and here there are several footbridges that cross the streams that run through the grove. These are generally seasonal, and have water only in the winter and spring.

The remaining two giants are at about 0.25 mile just before the trail leads through a gap in the second fallen sequoia. At the junction with Forest View Trail, stay left and continue on the Big Trees Interpretive Trail.

Follow the trail past several other stations, and return to Station 1 just before 0.5 mile. Have the children reread the information plaque to see how well they did identifying the trees and shrubs.

The interpretive trail leads back to the parking area at 0.5 mile, and the Forest View Trail leads off to the right just before the lot. Take this right turn to continue your hike.

This trail leads around the edge of the grove through old-growth forest, and in the first 0.25 mile crosses three seasonal creeks. The children will like to explore along the banks of these creeks for water animals if there is any water.

From 0.75 to 1 mile, the trail leads through an old-growth forest that rises high above as it filters out the sunlight. Have the children look for small plants that grow along the trail and talk about how they have become adjusted to living with little sunlight, and would likely perish if the old trees were downed for any reason.

The children can also keep an eye out for small animals such as squirrels and birds along here. After they fail to locate any down low, where they are likely to look, have them look near the tops of the canopy, where there is more light and food for the animals.

After crossing another creek at 1 mile, the trail curves back around to join the interpretive trail at about 1.25 miles. From there you can take the Big Trees Interpretive Trail either to the left or right to return to the parking area at 1.5 miles, where there are water, rest rooms, and a picnic area.

58. Indian Creek Trail

Type: Dayhike
Difficulty: Moderate for children
Distance: 3 miles, round trip
Hiking time: 3 hours
Elevation gain: Minimal
Hikable: Year-round
Map: US Forest Service

The canyon country of the North Fork of the American River is rugged, heavily forested, and hot in the middle of the summer. In general it can be inhospitable and threatening to beginning hikers, especially families with children. With its many tributaries draining steep gorges, there is no doubt the region can be daunting, but there are a number of hikes that can be enjoyed by families, and this is an excellent introductory hike to the gold rush region of Tahoe National Forest. Gold miners once flocked to the river and its tributaries in search of gold nuggets, and today there are still many people who mine the waterways for fun and profit. On any day you may encounter one or more of these modern-day miners as they pan and sluice for specks of gold dust. Children are always fascinated with even the idea of gold, and on this hike you can take along a small gold pan so the children can experience the fun, and hard work, that comes from gold panning.

Take I-80 east to just past Weimar, and take the Canyon Way exit; turn right on Canyon Way. Head south for about 1 mile to Yankee Jims Road and turn left. Stay on Yankee Jims Road until it becomes a dirt road, and continue for another 2.5 miles to the old suspension bridge where Yankee Jims Road crosses the North Fork of the American River. Park at the bridge and begin the trail at the confluence of Shirttail Creek and the North Fork. The trail heads up the east side of the river.

This trail is used regularly by miners working their mining claims along the North Fork, and they keep it in good condition for year-

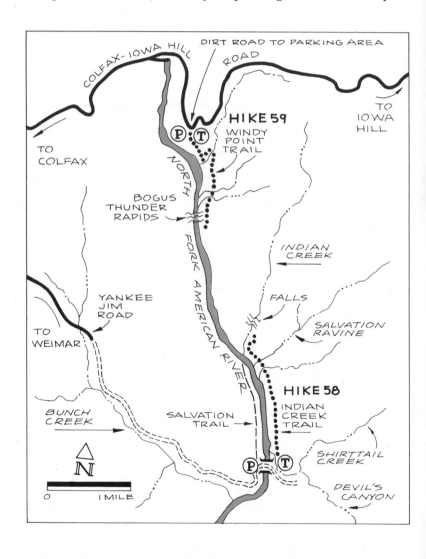

Even the smallest shady spot is a welcome relief from the sun on an open trail.

round hiking. The middle portion of the trail leads through the historic Salvation Bar mining claim, and you may want to read about some of the more famous claims in the region before you take the hike so you can discuss them as you walk along the trail.

You have to creek-hop over Shirttail Creek to begin the trail, and during high water you must be careful not to get wet.

As you cross the creek, have the children keep an eye out for large, flat outcroppings of bedrock where Native Americans once ground acorns and other seeds. You can identify these by the deep, round holes that were formed as the natives used pestles of hard stone to grind the seeds.

The first mile of the trail is level as it follows along uphill from the river. Large canyon live oaks furnish a canopy of shade so the trail is cool even on hot days. Wildflowers adorn the slopes during the spring bloom. You can both see and hear the river below as you hike along the trail.

Several small seasonal streams cross under the trail along this section, and children like to explore along their banks for frogs,

salamanders, and other small water animals when the water is flowing. The large, lush Indian rhubarb also grows along the creeks after
the winter rains.

At about 1.25 miles you cross one unnamed tributary, and then
Salvation Creek, before heading upstream on Indian Creek to several
pools of water beneath a 30-foot-high double waterfall. When the creek
is low, you can actually stand beneath the waterfall for a cooling
shower on warm days.

Return by the same route; however, in times of low water, you
can cross over the North Fork and return on Salvation Trail on the
west bank.

There is also a large, deep swimming hole with diving rocks and
a sandy beach on the north side of the river near the confluence of
Indian Creek and the North Fork.

59. Windy Point Trail

Type: Dayhike
Difficulty: Difficult for children
Distance: 3 miles, round trip
Hiking time: 3 hours
Elevation gain: 1,000 feet
Hikable: Year-round
Map: US Forest Service

This hike is much like the previous one (see hike 58, Indian Creek
Trail), except that it has a much steeper descent into the heart of
the North Fork Gorge and should not be attempted unless all members of the hiking party are in excellent condition; it should not be
attempted at all with children under the age of ten. There are great
views of the river gorge, and an occasional view of the river itself,
as you make the descent down into the gorge. This hike is a great
classroom where you can introduce your children to both the natural
and the human history of the region. Miners have hiked the trail for
well over 100 years, and the action of the river has been forming the
gorge for millions of years. The rarely seen water ouzel, which John
Muir said was his favorite bird in the Sierra Nevada, is known to
nest near the trail, and the unusual harlequin lupine (purple and
yellow blossoms) blooms near the mouth of side canyons in the spring.
You may want to read Muir's short essay "The Water Ouzel" before-

hand so the children can anticipate seeing this unusual bird.

Take I-80 east to Colfax and exit onto Clayton Way. Take the Colfax–Iowa Hill Road east off Clayton Way and follow it for 1 mile past the Mineral Bar Campground (see map on page 196). Two wooden posts mark a short dirt road on the right. Drive to the end of this road and park. The trail begins here, heading south.

The first section of the trail leads through a burned area where dense stands of chaparral have regrown to cover the barren slopes. Have the children keep an eye out to the left as you begin the descent. A large, fortresslike outcropping of rock known as Windy Point soon pops into view. Look for large raptors flying around the rocks; golden eagles have been reported nesting there.

The trail crosses a small feeder creek just before 0.5 mile, at which point the chaparral begins to give way to pine and oak (that is, unless another fire has devastated the area), and at about 1 mile a trail leads off to the right on a steep descent to the river. Continue on the main trail, which maintains a more gradual descent as it

Modern bridges take today's travelers far above the old gold-rush roads and trails.

passes by several side canyons and seasonal streams.

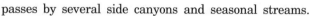

Have the children discuss the role they think fire plays in the natural world. They may think that all fires should be suppressed, and you can explain, as well as show, the regeneration that occurs after a major fire.

The trail winds in and out as it comes close to the river, moves away from it, and comes back again.

At about 1.25 miles the first of two tributaries feed into the North Fork. The first canyon mouth has a rocky floor and is full of aquatic creatures such as salamanders and frogs. It is also a place where you may be able to find specks of gold as you pan in the quiet waters around the rocks.

The second canyon mouth has a smooth, sandy floor where you and the children can look for the footprints of raccoons, deer, rabbit, skunk, coyote, and maybe even bobcat that come to the creek to drink. Above the mouth there is a grotto where lush ferns such as the large woodwardia grow.

The water ouzel has been known to nest on the rocky ledge across the river from the second canyon.

At 1.5 miles the trail ends near some rapids known as Bogus Thunder. This is a good place to rest and eat lunch before beginning the hot, steep climb back to the car. Be sure you have plenty of water for the climb out.

60. Bear Falls Trail Loop

Type: Overnight
Difficulty: Easy for children
Distance: 2 miles, loop
Hiking time: 2 hours
Elevation gain: 100 feet
Hikable: Year-round
Map: Placer County Parks Department

Bear River Park, a 250-acre county park on the banks of the Bear River, lies at about 1,800 feet elevation and has a wide diversity of plant and animal life. There are willow and alder near the river, ponderosa pine and Douglas fir along the hiking and equestrian trails, open grassland in the meadows, and chaparral on the exposed southern slopes. Signs of deer, raccoon, skunk, squirrel, porcupine, fox, and even a few bobcat can be found in the park, although you have to be quiet and observant to see these. The Bear River was one of the most productive streams for gold during the gold rush, and is still mined today, although it is rock aggregate that is mined from the river rather than gold.

From I-80 at Colfax, take Ben Taylor Road north to Tokayana Way. Turn left onto Tokayana Way and continue to Milk Ranch Road. Take the right fork at the junction of Tokayana Way and Milk Ranch Road and continue to the park entrance. Park at the picnic area parking lot, which is near the gravel road to the group camping area and walk-in campground.

From the picnic area parking lot, head south along the paved road for several hundred feet to the gravel road that leads off to the right. This road is closed to motor vehicles except for approved groups, and follows the river as it curves to the east.

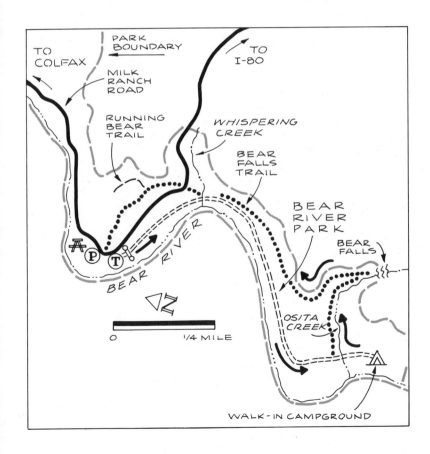

Many mountain streams have small waterfalls and ponds.

At about 0.25 mile Whispering Creek crosses the road and enters the river. The children like to explore along the bank of the creek, especially among the riparian forest of willow and alder near the river. Here they may find signs of many small animals that come to the creek for water, and see small birds that live in the low-lying trees.

The road continues along the river until just past 0.5 mile, and then turns away from the banks at about 0.75 mile. The road passes by the group camping area and crosses Osita Creek to the walk-in campground at just past 0.75 mile.

Except in very dry years there is potable water at the walk-in campground, which is first-come, first-served.

After you have set up camp, the children can explore along the river, looking for fish, frogs, tadpoles, and water-loving birds.

Bear Falls is accessible from the campground via a trail that follows along the north banks of Osita Creek, and is about 0.25 mile from the campground. This is a good after-dinner hike, especially in the winter and spring after heavy rains have filled the creek and the falls are thundering over the rocks.

For the return hike, take the Bear Falls Trail to the right from the campground as it follows Osita Creek upstream.

After viewing the falls at 0.25 mile (1 mile from the trailhead and parking lot), continue north on the Bear Falls Trail as it makes a sharp left turn near the falls, and heads through a canopy of ponderosa pine and Douglas fir uphill from the river.

At about 1.75 miles the trail rejoins the gravel road. Take a right on the road as it crosses over Whispering Creek, and then take a right on the trail as it leaves the road just past the creek.

Bear Falls Trail takes a sharp left turn away from the creek after about 100 feet, and crosses the paved Milk Ranch Road in another 200 feet.

Continue through the forest to just under 2 miles, where the trail forks. Take the left fork to return to the parking lot.

61. Hardrock Trail

Type: Dayhike
Difficulty: Moderate for children
Distance: 2 miles, loop
Hiking time: 1 hour
Elevation gain: 300 feet
Hikable: Year-round
Map: California Department of Parks and Recreation

The focus of Empire Mine State Historic Park is the old Empire Mine site and building remnants. There is an excellent visitor center, mine equipment exhibit, scale model of the old underground mine, and many buildings and building foundations from the heyday of the gold rush period. The Empire Mine was the oldest, largest, and richest gold mine in the Grass Valley district, which was home to many gold mines during the last half of the nineteenth century. In addition to the historic portion of the park, there is a 2-mile loop trail that takes hikers to the top of Osborne Hill, where there is an outstanding vista of the 700 acres in the park.

 Take I-80 east to Colfax, and exit onto Colfax Highway. Take a right onto East Empire Street and continue to the park. Park in the parking lot on the south side of the road.

Before beginning the Hardrock Trail, you can explore the visitor center and historic buildings of the mine. After walking around the buildings, including a formal garden area and reflecting pool, you can begin the Hardrock Trail near the New Rich mineshaft.

The trail leads past the carpenter shop and mine display and the foundation for the old lime shed before heading into the ponderosa pine forest at about 0.25 mile.

 Between 0.25 mile and 1 mile the trail winds around old mines and mine tailing piles where the children can see how much rock had to be removed from beneath the ground before any significant amount

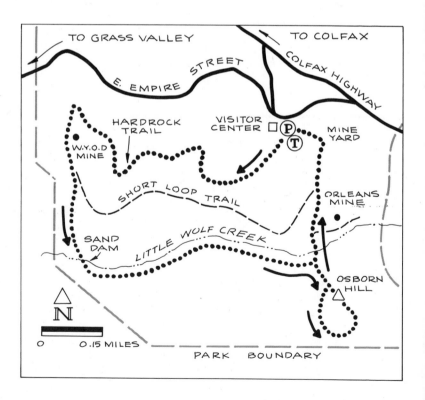

Even the youngest hikers stop to look at information posts.

of gold was discovered. Unlike placer mining, where individual miners could pan and sluice for gold nuggets and dust with little investment in equipment, hardrock mining required large numbers of miners operating large equipment. Have the children discuss why hardrock mines were owned and operated by large corporations or wealthy individuals rather than miners who filed small claims like those who worked the placer gold fields.

At just under 1 mile the Short Loop Trail leads off to the left. If anyone in your party is getting tired, you can take this shorter route back through the ponderosa pine forest for a hike of just over 1.5 miles.

For the hike described here, continue on the Hardrock Trail and by 1 mile it leads by a sand dam on the Little Wolf Creek. The children can play in and around the creek as you take a short break before continuing the loop.

Just past 1.5 miles a side trail leads off to the right. Take this short side trip to the top of Osborne Hill, reached at 1.25 miles, where you can look out over the entire Empire Mine area. Have the children point out various buildings and talk about how they were used.

From Osborne Hill loop around to the main trail as it leads on through the ponderosa forest back toward the historic mine area. About 50 yards after you rejoin the main trail, you cross the creek. In another 100 yards a trail leads to the right; stay left. You pass by several more sites where you can investigate mining debris, and in another 200 yards the other end of the Short Loop Trail comes in from the left; stay right. At just under 2 miles the trail reaches the end of the ore train tracks that brought the ore from beneath the earth to the surface, where the ore was crushed to separate the gold from the quartz.

---

62. South Yuba Independence Trail

Type: Dayhike
Difficulty: Moderate for children
Distance: 2.5 miles, round trip
Hiking time: 2 or 3 hours
Elevation gain: Minimal
Hikable: Year-round
Map: California Department of Parks and Recreation

This trail, located in South Yuba River Recreation Area, is a very unusual one. Most trails are either inaccessible to those who are handicapped or are very artificial and obviously made to be accessible. Sequoya Challenge, a non-profit group of volunteers concerned about wilderness access for the handicapped, has changed that. They have worked with the California Department of Parks and Recreation, and more than a dozen other groups, to build a trail that is not only accessible to all but also retains its wild flavor. On the South Yuba Independence Trail, everybody, including those who are wheelchair-bound or who require walkers, can experience the forest, river, and mountainsides on their own. The trail is perched on the side of the canyon of the Yuba River, and follows the gentle contour of the hills as it travels near abandoned gold mining flumes. The trail is wide, smooth, and never exceeds a 5 percent grade. The hard-packed clay can be slippery after a heavy rain, so it is best to call Sequoya Challenge (916-272-3823) or the South Yuba River Project (916-432-2546) for current trail conditions if it has rained shortly before you plan to hike.

Take I-80 east to Auburn and exit onto CA-49 north. Follow CA-49 to 6 miles north of Nevada City, to an asphalt pullout and parking area that is easy to miss. Look for blue parking signs on the east side of the highway. The trail leads both east and west from the parking area, but the hike described here heads to the west.

Have the children discuss why a special hiking trail has been developed for handicapped individuals. You may want to stress that

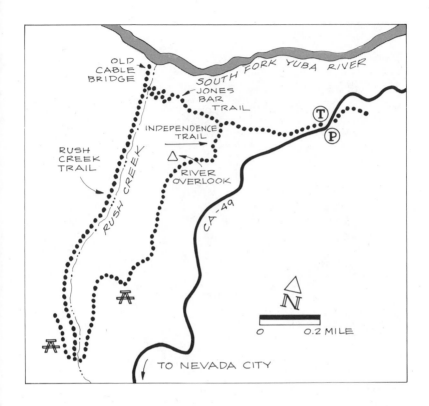

individuals with a wide variety of physical handicaps can still have a strong desire to have experiences in nature.

The trail leads back beneath the highway under a bridge where adults have to duck to get under. For the first 0.5 mile, the trail leads through a canopy of mixed conifer-oak-bay forest that provides plenty of shade on warm days. At about 0.3 mile a spur trail heads downhill on the right to a swimming hole at Jones Bar. You may want to use this on the return trip, particularly on warm days. The spur is about a 0.5-mile round trip with about a 300-foot drop in elevation to the river.

Between the trail spur and the overlook, there are also the remains of two gold rush flumes that carried water to hydraulic miners below. You may want to read up on hydraulic mining before taking the trip so the children know what the flumes were used for. Have the children discuss how miners used water in their efforts to uncover gold nuggets, flakes, and ore.

From the first river overlook just before 0.5 mile, you can look out over Jones Bar and the remains of an old cable bridge that once

An evening stroll along the Sacramento River is a perfect family outing.

crossed the river there. You can also see Rush Creek as it joins with the South Fork Yuba River.

There is a rest room just past the overlook.

After the overlook, the trail leads away from the river as it follows the contour of the hill into the side canyon formed by Rush Creek. Between 1 mile and 1.25 miles you pass by several other old flumes, and at 1.5 miles you come to Rush Creek, where the flume crosses over the creek. From here you have a great view of a waterfall during wet weather, and there is a fishing ramp that is made for handicapped anglers.

From here you can return to the parking area for a 2.5-mile round trip (or the Jones Bar Spur Trail for a side trip to the swimming hole for a total of 3 miles), or able persons can follow the 1-mile-long Rush Creek Trail down the creek until it joins with the South Fork Yuba River. From there you can hike back upriver to the swimming hole. This makes for about a 3.5-mile loop if you return by the Jones Bar Trail.

63. Bridgeport to Point Defiance Trail Loop

Type: Overnight
Difficulty: Moderate to difficult for children
Distance: 3 miles, loop
Hiking time: 4 hours
Elevation gain: 300 feet
Hikable: Year-round
Map: US Army Corps of Engineers

Englebright Lake lies behind the 260-foot-high and 1,142-foot-long Englebright Dam, constructed by the US Army Corps of Engineers to contain debris from hydraulic mining that had been clogging up the lower Yuba River, as well as the Sacramento River, for more than half a century. Since its completion in 1941, the reservoir has become a recreational destination for thousands of fishermen, boaters, and picnickers. Camping and hiking are not as big an attraction at the lake, for the steep slopes of the gorge where the dam was constructed make it difficult to build trails. Campgrounds are unusual around the lake, because all must be reached by boat or foot. A number of small campsites are located around the 24-mile-long shoreline of the lake, though, and one, on the tip of Point Defiance, is accessible by the only developed trail to the shore of the lake. This trail and campground is within the boundaries of the South Yuba River Recreation Area, though the trail begins in Bridgeport State Park.

Take CA-99 north to Yuba City, and then CA-20 east to Penn Valley. Take Pleasant Valley Road north from Penn Valley to Bridgeport State Park. Park in the parking lot by the old covered bridge. The trail begins on the east side of the South Fork Yuba River at the end of the bridge.

The bridge across the river is an unusual one. Built in 1862, its shake roof and sides have protected from deterioration the timbers that form the trusses and arches. At 243 feet, it is the longest of any covered bridge left in the world. One of only twelve left in California, it is also considered the most remarkable covered bridge in the United States.

After exploring the bridge as you hike across it, take a sharp left on a single-track trail that leads along the contour of the slope above the South Fork Yuba River below.

At about 0.25 mile there is a small beach that is accessible from

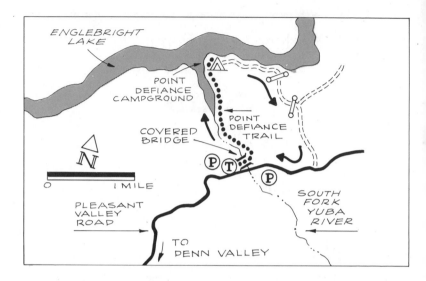

the trail, where the children can explore along the river's edge.

After the small beach, the trail moves uphill away from the river, until, near 0.5 mile, it drops back down toward a large gravel bar, where gold miners probably worked during gold rush times. Have the children try to imagine what it must have looked like with hundreds of miners using their pans and cradles to separate the gold nuggets and dust from the gravel and sand.

By 0.75 mile a side trail leads down to the sandbar and confluence of the South Fork Yuba River with the Yuba River. You may want to take this short side trip so the children can have a break as they explore around the edge of the river.

Return to the main trail and take a left to continue to the campsite, and by 0.9 mile you have reached the shore of Englebright Lake, where the mouth of the Yuba River is submerged by the high waters of the lake.

At 1 mile the trail forks and you can either go to the left down toward the lake or uphill to the right. To reach the campsite, take a right as the trail leads uphill into some rock outcroppings and boulders. The children may climb on these, but caution them to watch for rattlesnakes and poison oak.

You come to the campground at about 1.25 miles. This is a very small campground, and there may be people camping here if you come into the campground late in the day. This is unlikely if you are hiking in the off-season for boating, but if the campsite is occupied, you may talk to the other campers to see if you can share the site.

There is no potable water at the site, and you must either bring in your own water or purify the lake water by boiling or other means.

After setting up camp, you can head back to the sandbar area by the lower trail that leads along the shore of the lake. There are plenty of places along the shore of both the lake and the river for the children to wade, swim, or fish, as well as search for water animals. They can also use one of your plates to pan for gold.

For your return trip, you can either return by the same route, or make a loop by heading uphill from the campground. The hike described here leads uphill for the loop.

The trail out of the campground is a fire road that makes a steady climb. Along the roadbed there are boulders that jut out from the banks, and in some of them you can see dikes and sills (veins that run either vertically or horizontally) of quartz in the granite. These were once the primary sources of gold.

At about 1.4 miles there is a drainage area from above the road where you can see the power of running water. Large boulders have been moved by recent flooding. Have the children imagine what this area would look like with the water running full force down the hillside toward the lake below.

There is a much larger quartz dike at about 1.6 miles, one that may very well have held gold deposits.

This is the longest covered bridge left in the world.

Across the road are a number of small green shrubs that have bunches of small, white flowers in the spring and clumps of red berries in late summer and fall. These are toyon, and their berries were a food source for Native Americans who lived in the region.

The climb continues steadily uphill until about 2 miles, at which point you come to a gate that keeps out motor vehicles. The top of the ridge, which is about 300 feet above the lake below, is just past the gate.

The trail heads downhill for several hundred yards and crosses an open grass area that has plenty of colorful wildflowers between February or March and June.

Just past 2.1 miles you come to a cattle gate and hikers' stile. Go through the stile and at the T intersection turn right on the gravel road as it heads downhill.

The gravel road continues a sharp descent for about 0.75 mile as it drops down toward the South Fork Yuba River.

At 2.75 miles you reach Pleasant Valley Road, where you cross the road and turn right to continue downhill. At 3 miles you come to a parking lot on the left side of the road. If you would like to take a cooling swim, you can turn left into the parking lot and hike about 0.5 mile upriver to a popular swimming hole.

From the parking lot, cross back over the road and follow the trail to the covered bridge. Return to the parking area at 3.25 miles (about 4 miles if you take the side trip for swimming).

64. South Yuba Trail: Purdon Crossing

Type:	Dayhike
Difficulty:	Moderate for children
Distance:	3 miles, round trip
Hiking time:	3 hours
Elevation gain:	300 feet
Hikable:	Year-round
Map:	California Department of Water Resources

The South Fork Yuba River Canyon offers an unusual combination of recreational opportunities that are provided through the cooperation of a variety of state and federal agencies. The California Department of Parks and Recreation, US Bureau of Land Manage-

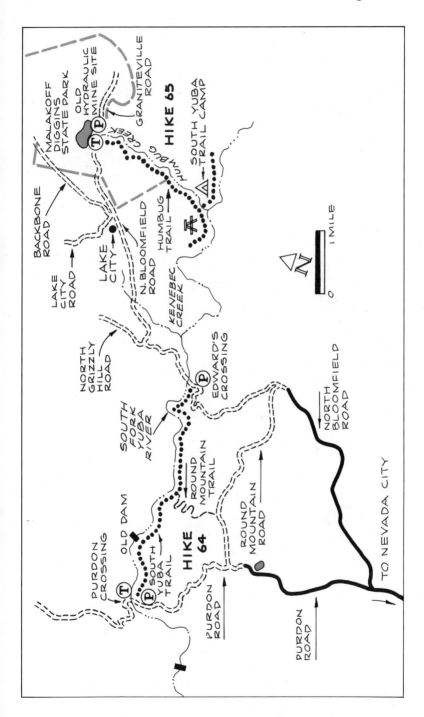

A perfect ending to a hot, dusty hike in the Sierra Nevada foothills

ment, US Forest Service, US Army Corps of Engineers, and California Department of Water Resources all offer recreational facilities within the region, and coordinate their efforts so well that visitors are often unaware that they have crossed jurisdictional boundaries. From swimming to white-water rafting to hiking, there is some activity along the river and its canyon for almost everyone. The previous two hikes (see hike 62, South Yuba Independence Trail, and hike 63, Bridgeport to Point Defiance Trail Loop) are also located within the South Fork Yuba River Recreation Area. Trail access to long stretches of the river is limited, but from Missouri Bar near Malakoff Diggins State Park to Purdon Crossing downstream north of CA-49, the South Yuba Trail has been completed and offers good access to the river.

Take I-80 east to Auburn, and CA-49 north to Nevada City. Take the Purdon–North Bloomfield Road just west of Nevada City. The road forks in about 1 mile. Take the left fork, Purdon Road, and continue to the parking area at Purdon Crossing. The last 2 miles of road are gravel. The trail begins about 50 yards east of the bridge, on the south side of the river.

During high water, this section of the river is a Class III–IV white-water run and a popular rafting area for experienced white-water rafters.

This new trail leads upstream along the river, with regular access by spur trails, through a canopy of oak and pine. Small streams, some spring-fed and year-round, cross the trail at intervals, and children like to explore among the ferns and other small water-loving plants for small aquatic animals and insects. Frogs and salamanders are often out and about during the early summer.

The trail passes the remains of an old dam (not visible during high water) at about 1 mile. During low water you can head down to the river to explore around the foundation of the dam, and maybe do a little panning in water pockets around some of the rocks.

While exploring around the dam area, have the children look for evidence of how powerful the rushing waters of the river are at runoff. Point out to them the large boulders along the river that have been moved by the roaring waters, and look for trees that have been toppled and possibly moved downstream.

At just past 1.5 miles the Round Mountain Trail comes in from the right. Soon after this junction, the South Yuba Trail loses its canopy and becomes exposed to the hot canyon sun. You can continue all the way to Edward's Crossing for a 3.5-mile one-way hike (shuttle a vehicle to the parking area here) or a 7-mile round trip.

For the hike described here, you turn around at the Round Mountain Trail junction and return by the same route for a 3-mile round trip. You can have a rest and lunch break beside the river.

For a winter hike, when you would want the exposure to the sun, you can begin this hike at Edward's Crossing and hike downstream to the Round Mountain Trail junction for a 4-mile round trip. To get to the parking area at Edward's Crossing, stay right on North Bloomfield Road when it forks with Purdon Road. The last 2.5 miles are unpaved.

65. Humbug Trail

Type: Overnight
Difficulty: Difficult for children
Distance: 5 miles, round trip
Hiking time: 5 hours
Elevation gain: 1,200 feet
Hikable: Year-round
Map: California Department of Water Resources

Malakoff Diggins State Park is the site of an old mining town and of the best examples of hydraulic mining left in the gold country. Gold was mined in several ways during the heyday of the gold rush. The easiest and most popular was placer mining, where individual miners panned and sluiced for gold nuggets and dust along streams and rivers where gold had settled after gold-bearing quartz deposits upstream had been eroded away. The heavier gold settled to the bottom of streams as the water rushed downhill. After these deposits ran out, most miners turned to hardrock mining, where they had to dig deep underground to find gold-bearing quartz veins. They blasted these large veins into smaller rocks and brought them to the surface, where they were crushed and the gold nuggets and dust were separated from the rest of the ore. Other miners, however, decided to assist nature in the erosion process, and proceeded to develop huge nozzles that literally washed away hillsides. They captured the gravel and dirt as it washed down from the hillsides and sent it through large sluices to separate the gold from the rocks and sand. This was called hydraulic mining, and the museum at Malakoff Diggins explains it in detail. This hike begins near the largest remaining example of this process, and you may want to hike the 2-mile loop around the headwaters of Humbug Creek, where hydraulic mining was used to erode whole mountainsides away, after you return to your vehicle.

For directions, see the previous hike (hike 64, South Yuba Trail: Purdon Crossing; map on page 213). When the Purdon–North Bloomfield Road forks less than 1 mile west of Nevada City, take the right fork, onto North Bloomfield Road. Continue on it past Edward's Crossing and Lake City into the park, reached about 4.5 miles after crossing the river. Park in the parking area at the Humbug Trailhead. The old hydraulic mining area is on the north side of the road, and the Humbug Trail leads downhill on the south side.

During the latter part of the nineteenth century, gold miners hiked up and down Humbug Creek panning for gold that had not been caught by the large sluices used in the hydraulic mining above and instead had settled along the creek as it dropped down to the South Yuba River some 1,200 feet below. Today the trail they used is one of four access trailheads to the river between the town of Washington and CA-49.

The trail leads down through a mixed canopy of oak, pine, and fir. There are a number of ponderosa pine in the forest at the top of the trail, but these disappear as the trail drops down to lower elevations.

Children like to explore along the banks of the creek as they hike down the trail looking for the larvae of aquatic insects such as caddis flies and mayflies. These larvae build cocoons of small sticks or pebbles, and attach themselves to the underside of rocks along the edge of the stream. Anglers use these as bait when fishing for trout. There are also small pools of water with tadpoles, water skippers, and other small animals that children like to watch.

In some of the stretches of the creek where it does not drop so quickly, the water settles into small pools where sand collects around larger rocks. These are excellent places to use a camping plate or drinking cup to pan for gold dust. Even if you don't find any, the children get excited about the prospect. The museum at Malakoff Diggins State Park even provides pans and small glass containers for collecting any dust you may find.

At 2 miles the trail reaches the Humbug picnic site on the banks of the river. This is a good place to take a break before heading upstream to the South Yuba Trail campsite at 2.5 miles.

After you have set up camp, the children can explore along the banks of the river, but caution them about the swift current during times of high water.

The campground sits high above the river, with several gravel terraces leading down to the river. Caution everyone about rattlesnakes; they are common here.

Return to the parking area by the same route. On hot days, be sure you take plenty of water (none is available at the campground and you will have to purify water from the river and creek before drinking it).

Also, on the way down you may keep an eye out for pools along the creek where the children can wade or take a dip on the way back up. This will break up the long climb out, and give everyone a pleasant break on hot days.

Index

About the author:

Sebastopol, California, resident Bill McMillon has been exploring the outdoors since his boyhood days in Mississippi. A teacher, counselor and administrator in California and Arizona for seventeen years, Bill now writes full time, and is the author of *Best Hikes With Children: San Francisco's North Bay, Best Hikes With Children: San Francisco's South Bay* (also from The Mountaineers), *California's Underwater State Parks—A Diver's Guide, Volunteer Vacations,* and *Nature Nearby,* among others. He credits his 10-year-old son Kevin, an enthusiastic hiking companion, as co-author of this book.

Other books you may enjoy from The Mountaineers:

Best Short Hikes In and Around the North Sacramento Valley,
Soares. 75 day hikes within an hour's drive of the Valley. Includes
Castle Crags, Shasta Lake, Whiskeytown Lake, McArthur-Burney
Falls, Hat Creek and Pit River, Yolla Bollys and Coast Range,
Redding, Anderson, Red Bluff, Chico, and Oroville.

Best Hikes With Children: San Francisco's North Bay,
McMillon.
Guide to 90 day hikes in the North Bay area. Includes trail directions and details, safety, flora and fauna, hiking with kids, and
more. Maps and photos.

Best Hikes With Children: San Francisco's South Bay,
McMillon. Guide to 85 day hikes in the South Bay area. Hike descriptions feature information on distance, difficulty and elevation
gain, plus notes on flora and fauna. Maps and photos.

**Best Short Hikes in California's Northern Sierra: A Guide
to Day Hikes Near Campgrounds,** Whitehill.
Details on 74 hikes around between the San Joaquin/Mammoth
area and Donner Pass. Includes information on campgrounds and
their facilities, hike distance, difficulty, starting and high points,
maps, and photos.

Best Hikes With Children in Western and Central Oregon,
Henderson.
100 easily accessible hikes, many lesser-known, with detailed trail
information. Tips on hiking with kids, safety, and wilderness eth-
ics.

Day Hikes From Oregon's Campgrounds, Ostertag.
Guide to campgrounds that access the best hikes and nature walks
in Oregon. Facilities, hike descriptions, more.

**Exploring Oregon's Wild Areas: A Guide for Hikers, Back-
packers, X-C Skiers & Paddlers,** Sullivan. Detail-stuffed guide-
book to Oregon's 65 wilderness areas, wildlife refuges, nature preserves, and state parks.

Available from your local bookstore or outdoor store, or from The
Mountaineers Books, 1001 SW Klickitat Way, Suite 201, Seattle,
WA 98134. Send or call for our catalog of more than 300 outdoor
titles: 1-800-553-4453.

THE MOUNTAINEERS, founded in 1906, is a nonprofit outdoor activity and conservation club, whose mission is "to explore, study, preserve, and enjoy the natural beauty of the outdoors. . . ." Based in Seattle, Washington, the club is now the third-largest such organization in the United States, with 15,000 members and five branches throughout Washington State.

The Mountaineers sponsors both classes and year-round outdoor activities in the Pacific Northwest, which include hiking, mountain climbing, ski-touring, snowshoeing, bicycling, camping, kayaking and canoeing, nature study, sailing, and adventure travel. The club's conservation division supports environmental causes through educational activities, sponsoring legislation, and presenting informational programs. All club activities are led by skilled, experienced volunteers, who are dedicated to promoting safe and responsible enjoyment and preservation of the outdoors.

The Mountaineers Books, an active, nonprofit publishing program of the club, produces guidebooks, instructional texts, historical works, natural history guides, and works on environmental conservation. All books produced by The Mountaineers are aimed at fulfilling the club's mission.

If you would like to participate in these organized outdoor activities or the club's programs, consider a membership in The Mountaineers. For information and an application, write or call The Mountaineers, Club Headquarters, 300 Third Avenue West, Seattle, Washington 98119; (206) 284-6310.

Send or call for our catalog of more than 300 outdoor titles:

 The Mountaineers Books
1001 SW Klickitat Way, Suite 201
Seattle, WA 98134
1-800-553-4453